# Laura Ingalls Wilder

## *Real-Life Pioneer of the Little House Books*

Carin T. Ford

**Enslow Publishers, Inc.**

40 Industrial Road          PO Box 38
Box 398               Aldershot
Berkeley Heights, NJ 07922    Hants GU12 6BP
USA                           UK

http://www.enslow.com

**Library of Congress Cataloging-in-Publication Data**

Ford, Carin T.
    Laura Ingalls Wilder : real-life pioneer of the Little House books / Carin T. Ford.
      p. cm. — (People to know)
    Summary: Discusses the life and career of Laura Ingalls Wilder, famed author of
the "Little House" books.
    Includes bibliographical references and index.
    ISBN 0-7660-2105-X (hardcover)
      1. Wilder, Laura Ingalls, 1867–1957—Juvenile literature. 2. Authors,
American—20th century—Biography—Juvenile literature. 3. Women pioneers—
United States—Biography—Juvenile literature. 4. Frontier and pioneer life—United
States—Juvenile literature. 5. Children's stories—Authorship—Juvenile literature.
[1. Wilder, Laura Ingalls, 1867-1957. 2. Authors, American. 3. Women—
Biography.] I. Title. II. Series.
PS3545.I342 Z645    2003
813'.52—dc21
                                                 2002153085

Printed in the United States of America

10 9 8 7 6 5 4 3 2 1

**To Our Readers:**
We have done our best to make sure all Internet Addresses in this book were active and
appropriate when we went to press. However, the author and the publisher have no con-
trol over and assume no liability for the material available on those Internet sites or on
other Web sites they may link to. Any comments or suggestions can be sent by e-mail
to comments@enslow.com or to the address on the back cover.

Every effort has been made to locate all copyright holders of material used in this book.
If any errors or omissions have occurred, corrections will be made in future editions of
this book.

# Contents

*Laura Ingalls Wilder*

# On the Move

The Ingalls family was on the move—again. Huddled under blankets in the back of the covered wagon sat Laura and her sisters Mary and Carrie. It was February 1874, and it was not easy keeping warm as the frigid winds blew through the woods of Wisconsin.

The wagon traveled westward at a slow pace, almost a walk. Charles and Caroline Ingalls—called Ma and Pa by the girls—rode up front, guiding a team of horses. Underneath the wagon trotted Jack, a sturdy bulldog with dark streaks running across his fur.

It was not the first time Pa had packed up his family. Laura was used to riding in the covered wagon. She had just turned seven, but she had already moved three times. Like her father, Laura seemed to thrive on journeying to new places and seeing new things.

The wagon rolled on, making its way across frozen Lake Pepin. Once the Ingalls family crossed the lake—actually a wide section of the Mississippi River—they would be in Minnesota. Pa hoped to settle on the wide, grassy prairie there. He was an excellent carpenter, but he also loved the land. He was looking forward to plowing the rich Minnesota soil and growing wheat.

The Ingalls family was one of hundreds of families that packed their belongings in a covered wagon and moved west in the late 1800s. Land was cheap out west—acres and acres of it. Pioneers had every reason to hope they would make their fortune in Wisconsin, Minnesota, Kansas, Nebraska, or Oregon. Word spread that prairie soil was good soil, with few trees or rocks. These grasslands sounded perfect for farming.

"It was such a new world, reaching to the far horizon without break of tree or chimney stack," said one pioneer, "just sky and grass and grass and sky. . . ."[1]

The pioneers also faced great hardships. Prairie winters could be deadly, with blizzards that often lasted for days at a time. There were droughts, fires, poisonous snakes, hailstorms, and outbreaks of diseases such as smallpox, measles, dysentery, and typhoid. Troubles arose with the Indians who had lived on this land for centuries. They were angry that the United States government was pushing them away to make room for the new settlers.

In addition, most settlers lived miles from their nearest neighbors. Some gave up in despair. They could not stand the loneliness. One pioneer wrote across the door of his abandoned cabin, "250 miles to the nearest post office, 100 miles to wood, 20 miles to water, 6 inches to hell. Gone to live with wife's folks."[2]

But the Ingalls family, like many pioneers, found the idea of cheap land and wide-open spaces impossible to resist. Laura later wrote that her father wanted to move to a part of the country where wild animals could live without being afraid.

So covered wagons just like Laura's continued rolling across the country. In 1842, two hundred pioneers journeyed west. Eight years later, that number jumped to fifty-five thousand.

The wagon became Laura's home. "We rode in the covered wagon all day long, every day," she wrote.[3]

Only twelve feet long and four feet wide, the Ingalls wagon was made of hardwood with a canvas top. Caulk and tar kept the frame waterproof, while oil was used to rainproof the canvas top. The wagon held everything the family needed to survive the long journey—skillets, kettles, lanterns, linens, axes, guns, and ammunition.

Books, which Ma read aloud to the family at night, were carefully wrapped. Pa's fiddle was packed in its box and then wrapped in blankets to protect it from the jolting of the wagon.

Most important was food, such as flour, salt, sugar, beans, yeast, and bacon. Laura liked stopping for meals. Her father would build a small fire, and her mother would fry salt pork or cook bacon and pancakes, which they ate with molasses. Laura was old enough to help clean up when the meal was over.

*Like these pioneers in 1866, Laura and her family traveled west in a covered wagon.*

She washed the dishes in a bucket and then stored them in a box.

The best time, though, was after dinner. Laura sat around the campfire with her mother and sisters, and they listened to Pa play his fiddle. It was honey brown with silver flowers on the tailpiece. Sometimes Pa sang as he played. Laura's favorite songs were "Auld Lang Syne," "Pop Goes the Weasel," "Annie Laurie," "Bonny Doon," and "Home Sweet Home." The girls often fell asleep at night to the mellow sounds of their father's fiddling.

"It's the first thing I remember, Pa's playing us to sleep when we were little," Laura recalled years later. "He played the fiddle by the campfire at night. . . . We

never could—I see it now, though I didn't then—
we never could have gotten through it all without
Pa's fiddle."[4]

The wagon crossed Lake Pepin and continued west
across Minnesota. Pa's brother Peter was making the
journey with his family, too. Because it was so bitterly
cold that time of year, Pa and his brother decided
their families should camp out in an empty cabin
until the weather became warmer.

Yet the stay was only temporary. Soon, the wagon
would be packed up and the Ingalls family would be
on the move again.

♦ ♦ ♦ ♦ ♦

More than half a century later, Laura's experiences as a pioneer girl would be known throughout
the country. She would become the beloved author of
a set of stories called the *Little House* books.

Although not strictly autobiographical, the series
included many events that actually happened to
Laura and her family. In the *Little House* books, Laura
changed some names, invented or renamed some
people, and juggled dates. She referred to herself as
"Laura" or "she," telling about her experiences indi-
rectly, as if they had happened to someone else. In
her letters and diaries, published after she became
famous, Laura wrote more directly, using "I" as she
talked about her experiences.

Considered historical fiction, the *Little House*
books take readers on the journey with the Ingalls
family as they traveled in their covered wagon
through the untamed wilderness of America.

*Laura was born in this log cabin near Pepin, Wisconsin.*

# Growing Up

Laura Elizabeth Ingalls was born on February 7, 1867, in Pepin County, Wisconsin. Her first home was a log cabin deep in the "Big Woods" of the Chippewa River Valley region, not far from the Mississippi River. Bears, panthers, wolves, and deer roamed throughout the area. One of Laura's earliest memories was of this cabin and of her mother, father, and sister Mary, who was two years older than Laura.

The Ingallses were a pioneer family. Laura's father, Charles Ingalls, came from New York. Born in 1836, he was one of nine surviving children of a large family. When Pa was still a young boy, they packed up and moved to the Illinois prairie. Pa's family remained in Illinois for eight years and then headed west to

Wisconsin. They settled on a farm in Jefferson County near the Oconomowoc River.

Pa quickly learned to be a farmer, and a hard-working one at that. Whenever he and his brothers had the chance, they would work on neighboring farms as well as their own. Pa also learned how to be a carpenter, trapper, woodsman, and hunter.

Pa was able to attend school, but only when he was not needed on the farm. Pa was a good speller and enjoyed reading. At the age of seventeen, he spent $1.25—a sum he had worked hard for—to buy a set of books called *The Life of Napoleon.*

There was time for fun, too. Pa ice-skated on the frozen river in the winter and went to hot maple sugar parties, cornhusking parties, sleigh rides, and dances. Pa usually played his fiddle at the dances and harvest parties.

Any party was an excuse for the young people in the neighborhood to get together. Often, Charles saw Caroline Quiner, whose family lived on a farm on the other side of the Oconomowoc River.

Caroline—who would one day become Laura's "Ma"—was said to be the first non-Indian baby born in Milwaukee County, Wisconsin. Born in 1839, she had a difficult childhood. Ma was one of seven chil-dren, and when she was five, her father died.

Her mother moved her large family to a farm on the Oconomowoc River when Ma was nine. Without a father, the family had little money. Like Pa, Ma grew up knowing the value of hard work. She was respon-sible for helping to care for her younger siblings, sewing, cooking, and making sure plenty of food was prepared and stored to see them through the winter.

The following year, her mother married Frederick Holbrook, who added acreage to the farm and stability to their family life.

The Ingalls and Quiner families—living just across the river from each other and having lots of children between them—became good friends. In fact, three sets of Ingallses and Quiners got married. One pair was Pa and Ma. She was a schoolteacher when they met.

Shortly after their marriage, the couple moved west across the state to Pepin County. This was called the Big Woods district of Wisconsin, and it is where Laura was born.

Some of Pa's sisters and brothers, along with his parents, had also made the westward journey. The numerous aunts, uncles, and cousins spent a good deal of time together.

The log cabin where Laura's family lived was small. There, Laura and Mary passed many pleasant hours, popping corn in the fireplace and listening to Pa's fiddle music.

From the start, Laura was an active child, full of courage, curiosity, and energy. "I was a regular little tomboy," she later wrote.[1]

Her father had several nicknames for Laura, including "Little Half-Pint" and "Flutterbudget."[2] A special, lifelong bond developed between Laura and her father, whom she described as a strong yet gentle man.

Pa spent his days trapping animals so he would be able to trade the fur pelts when he went into Pepin. He also spent much of his time chopping down trees in the forest. He needed to make sure the family would have enough wood to burn during the long, cold winter. Most important, he hunted so that there would be enough meat for his wife and children.

Still, Pa was not content in the Big Woods. That section of Wisconsin was attracting more and more people. Although Ma liked having neighbors nearby, Pa did not enjoy hearing the sounds of other men's axes in the forest. He read advertisements telling of thousands of acres of available land out west. He missed wide-open spaces. Pa was ready to move.

Reluctant as Ma may have been, she agreed with her husband's decision to head to the prairie. "My parents possessed the spirit of the frontier," Laura said many years later.[3]

Not long after Laura turned one, Pa sold his farm to Gustaf Rejnhalt Gustafson, a settler from Sweden. Gustafson agreed to pay for the land in regular installments. Henry and Polly Quiner, Laura's uncle and aunt, sold their property as well. With their children, they too would make the journey.

After spending several days with Pa's parents, Laura's family was ready to load the covered wagon. Jack, the bulldog, took his place underneath it.

Traveling south through Iowa, Pa knew his destination. Although he had never laid eyes on it, he had purchased property in Missouri. He and Henry had each paid $900 for eighty acres of land.

The covered wagons crawled south and west until they came to Yellow Creek in Missouri. A couple of miles beyond the village of Rothville was Pa's homestead.

This was the Missouri prairie, with trees dotting the

land along the creeks and rivers. Pa decided to build his house by the creek. He also began farming the land. He needed to get to work right away before winter came.

Like most homes on the prairie, the house where Laura lived with her family was isolated. There were no neighbors, no houses nearby. The Ingallses were on their own. Pa delighted in knowing this. Ma was less sure.

Little has been documented about the family's stay in Missouri. Laura was only two years old. She could not remember anything of that time, much less write it down.

It *is* known that the family's stay in Missouri was short. Although it is unclear why, Pa and Henry decided to move on. Henry and Polly would travel north, returning to the Big Woods of Wisconsin. Pa wanted to go west.

So, in the fall of 1869, the covered wagons were loaded once again. Laura and Mary took their places in the back. They were heading to a place with end-less stretches of treeless grasslands and a scarcity of rivers and lakes. This was Kansas, and it was believed that only American Indians, native to the land, could survive in Kansas.

Before it became a state in 1861, Kansas had been part of the Louisiana Purchase. President Thomas Jefferson had bought the enormous area of land from the French in 1803, doubling the size of the United States at that time. It included much of the western part of the country. The U.S. government had originally designated Kansas as Indian territory. White settlers were not allowed to live there.

*"My parents possessed the spirit of the frontier," said Laura. Growing up, Charles Ingalls and Caroline Quiner Ingalls learned the vast array of skills they would need as American pioneers.*

But as the population of the United States increased, so did the need for more land. The country looked westward, and in 1854 Congress passed a law that allowed white settlers to move to the Kansas and Nebraska territories. Like Pa, many pioneers could not resist the nearly 50 million acres of unsettled prairie.

That section of the country was made even more enticing seven years later when President Abraham Lincoln supported the Homestead Act. For a $14 filing fee, a settler could acquire 160 acres of land. If he built a house there and lived on the land for five years, it was his.

Once considered an area of wild beasts, dust, and deserts, Kansas now attracted droves of newcomers. They hoped to make their fortunes as well as enjoy the freedom of all that available land.

Years later, Laura described traveling west in a covered wagon as largely pleasant. In her *Little House* books, she told of snuggling under blankets while the wagon rolled along. She wrote of her mother cooking corn cakes and salt pork over an open fire, and her father playing his fiddle under the stars.

In her books, Laura gave an idealized account of the trip west. In reality, the journey could be extremely difficult.

Dust was everywhere, covering the pioneers' skin as thickly as the endless swarms of fleas and mosquitoes. Sudden rainstorms turned the dirt trails to mud, making it impossible for the wagon wheels to turn. Clothing and linens were soaked in the downpours.

River crossings cost hundreds of pioneers their lives, as they fell off the wagons and drowned. Others died in buffalo stampedes or were killed instantly if they fell beneath the wagon wheels.

"A little boy fell over the front end of the wagon during our journey," wrote pioneer Edward Lenox. "In his case, the great wheels rolled over the child's head—crushing it to pieces."[4]

Lightning killed many travelers, and hailstones as large as apples caused numerous injuries. When illnesses struck, there were no medical supplies.

Of the more than half million pioneers who traveled across the country in the 1800s, one in ten died along the way. Their gravestones dotted the trails west.

Still, Laura described the wagon journey as an adventure. "You never know what will happen next, nor where you'll be tomorrow, when you are traveling in a covered wagon," she wrote.[5]

Across the Verdigris River was the town of Independence, Kansas. Pa drove the team of horses—Pet and Patty, the girls had named them—another thirteen miles west. When he came to Walnut Creek, Pa decided he was home.

The area Pa had picked for his homestead was actually part of a reservation for the Osage Indians. Pa never filed a claim on the land, so he may not have known that he was not allowed to settle there. It is also possible that Pa assumed the U.S. government was taking over the land and the Indians would soon be gone.

At the time the Ingallses arrived at Walnut Creek, the Osage were away on a hunting trip. Like many Indians, they were a nomadic tribe whose lifestyle was based on hunting for food. Depending on the time of year, the Indians hunted bison, deer, elk, bear, and smaller animals.

The Osage originally lived in Missouri. Then, in 1808, the U.S. government had started taking their land to open up the area to white settlers. So in 1825, the Osage were forced into a small section of Kansas. Although the Osage had numbered 17,000 in 1680, their population had dwindled to 3,500 by 1860.

According to Laura, her father respected the Indians. He seemed to understand how difficult it was for them to be forced off their homeland. Her mother, however, was afraid of them.

Indians frequently visited the family's cabin while Pa was out hunting. Noiselessly, they would appear in the doorway of the cabin. They seemed to be looking for food, and Ma would offer them cornbread. After a while, they would leave.

For Ma—and other settlers—it was an uneasy existence. The Osage had freely roamed the vast grasslands for years. They resented being shoved onto a small reservation where, even now, white settlers insisted on living. When they returned from hunting trips, the Indians often found their homes had been burned to the ground, their trees cut down, and their fields plowed over.

Frequent skirmishes took place between the settlers and the Indians, in spite of the fact that the land legally belonged to the Indians. In retaliation, the Indians stole livestock, tore down the settlers' cabins, and burned harvested hay. The settlers went after the Indians with their guns.

The pioneers' isolated existence on the prairie only

added to Ma's fears for her family's safety. The closest neighbor was about a mile away.

Another settler, Eliza Wyckoff, had come from Ohio and lived ten miles from the Ingalls cabin. She recalled feeling frightened when Osage Indians came to her house. One morning, six braves arrived at her door:

> *They stayed about half an hour, and laughed and talked to each other. I sat in the back part of the house and felt very uncomfortable. I could not understand anything they said and felt very much relieved when they left.*[6]

When the U.S. government offered the Osage a new treaty, the Indians needed to make a decision. Should they fight for their land or should they accept the terms of the treaty? The initial treaty offered the Osage twenty cents an acre for more than eight million acres of the Osage reservation. This ridiculously low price was eventually raised to $1.25 an acre. If the Osage accepted the offer, they would move to a new reservation in Oklahoma.

Laura wrote about hearing the Indians' angry war whoops night after night, while her father stood guard with a gun: "Every night the Indian drums beat faster, faster, and the wild yipping rose higher and higher, faster, wilder."[7]

Pa explained to Laura and Mary that the chanting and drumming coming from the nearby campsite was the Indians' way of talking about war.

Would the Osage leave the area . . . or would the white settlers be the ones to go? Many families would be affected by the decision. In 1868, there were close to fifteen thousand white settlers on Osage lands.

One morning the war cries abruptly ended. There would be no war between the Indians and the settlers, Pa told Laura. The Osage signed a treaty giving up any claim to their land. They would leave Kansas and move to Oklahoma.

Laura described watching the seemingly endless procession of Indians ride slowly along the trail by her cabin. The line stretched to the east and west as far as she could see. The Indians were leaving the Kansas prairie forever.

At the same time, Pa received a letter saying that Gustaf Gustafson, the man who had bought their farm in Wisconsin, wanted to stop making his payments on the land. He wanted Pa to take back the farm.

Pa felt it would be best if the family moved back to Wisconsin. They could return to their old farm. They could leave their complicated situation in Kansas.

It had been a hard year for the Ingallses. Besides the uneasy situation with the Osage, the family had suffered from malaria. Laura referred to the illness as "fever 'n' ague." Carried by mosquitoes, malaria is a disease that causes fever and chills. Dr. George Tann, an African-American doctor who worked in Kansas among the Osage, treated the Ingalls family with a bitter medicine called quinine. Everyone recovered.

There was another mouth to feed, as well. In August 1870, Ma gave birth to a third child, Caroline Celestia. She would always be called Carrie.

Shortly after Carrie's birth, a U.S. census taker came to the township. He listed Pa as C. P. Ingles, a thirty-four-year-old carpenter. Ma was thirty and her occupation was "Keeping House." Mary's age was five, Laura's three, and Carrie's two weeks. The place where the census taker was supposed to list the value of the Ingalls property was left blank. At that time, Pa did not legally own the homestead.

Ma worried that they had wasted the year building a log cabin and barn, plowing the fields to ready them for planting crops, and digging a well for fresh water. Had it all been for nothing?

Pa and Ma packed the covered wagon with supplies and began the trip north.

# 3

# Back to the Big Woods

Laura and Mary stared out the back of the wagon as they left Kansas behind. Carrie sat on her mother's lap up front. This would be a long journey, traveling east into Missouri and then north into Iowa before finally arriving in Wisconsin.

The covered wagon was loaded with provisions: dried beef, flour, cornmeal, and beans. There were pots, pans, forks, knives, clothing, linens, and, of course, Pa's fiddle.

Unlike some pioneers, the Ingallses did not travel with their furniture. The wagons were heavy enough. The horses could pull the wagons only fifteen or twenty miles before they needed to rest for the night. Besides, Pa was an excellent carpenter and was always able to make chairs and beds. Laura's family did pack straw mattresses, which the girls sat on during the day. At night, the family was able to sleep on them in the wagon instead of lying on the hard ground.

Once, when Pa needed to cross a flooded stream, he led his horses into the water with the wagon floating behind. He jumped into the surging water to help guide the animals while Ma took the reins. It was a dangerous crossing, and Laura recalled feeling sick to her stomach as the wagon jerked and jolted in the creek.

Finally, the wagon made it to the other bank. Everyone—and everything—was dripping, but they were safely across.

As the wagon made its way into Missouri, Pa knew he would have to find work before continuing. He had little money and the food supply was low. When Pa found an abandoned cabin, he moved the family into it and began working for the cabin's owner.

Pa finally earned enough money to buy the necessary supplies. Before resuming the journey, he traded Pet and Patty for two larger horses. Pet and Patty were too small for the long and difficult trip.

The wagon continued northward and the Ingalls family reached Lake Pepin, Wisconsin, in May 1871. From there, it was only a short ride to the little log cabin in the Big Woods where Laura had been born.

The cabin was not empty. Gustaf Gustafson had not yet begun his journey west and was still living there. So Laura's family moved in for a while with her Uncle Henry, Aunt Polly, and their children. Laura played with her cousins Louisa, Charley, Albert, and Lottie.

*The pioneers traveling in this covered wagon packed everything from their furniture to their spinning wheel. The Ingalls family always left their chairs and beds behind—Pa built new ones wherever they settled.*

She was, in fact, happy to be around much of her extended family. She liked being with Aunt Eliza, Uncle Peter, and their children Peter, Alice, Ella, and Edith. She saw her Uncle Tom Quiner and spent a lot of time with Pa's parents, Grandma and Grandpa Ingalls.

Before long, Gustafson left for the West. Laura's family was able to move back into their old cabin, and Pa began farming the land that summer. It was a particularly hot and dry time in the Midwest. Without rain, creeks dried up and fires often broke out. A few hundred miles away in Chicago, an enormous fire spread more than three miles across the city, taking three hundred lives. This disaster became known as the Great Chicago Fire of 1871. There was also a fire where Laura lived, but her family's land was unharmed. Still, the weather remained dangerously hot and dry as the summer wore on.

Mary was sent to school for the summer session, which ran from May through July. Four-year-old Laura stayed at home with her mother. She helped Ma wash the dishes and make the beds. Laura also learned how to sew, knit, make cheese and soap, and grow fruits and vegetables, which could then be stored for the winter.

Although she kept busy, Laura enviously watched Mary head off to the Barry Corner School each morning with her cousins Louisa and Lottie. It was a long day without her sister to keep her company. But at least Laura had the evenings to look forward to. Then, Mary would teach Laura the new words she had learned to read that day.

The Barry Corner School was a log schoolhouse a short distance from the Ingalls cabin. Like most frontier schools, it had just one room. The teacher, Annie Barry, worked with the younger students during the summer. That summer of 1871, there were nineteen children attending the school.

Students were given a basic education, enough to help them get by in life. After all, education was a luxury to most pioneers. It was more important to know how to plow the soil and store food than it was to learn grammar. But many settlers soon realized that arithmetic was needed to keep business accounts. Reading and writing were needed for reading newspapers and handling land deeds.

Most frontier teachers taught reading, writing, spelling, grammar, and arithmetic. If the teacher had a map or a globe, geography and history might be included.

Laura's mother felt strongly that her girls should receive an education. She had once been a schoolteacher, and she knew education would help her daughters accomplish more in life.

In October, Laura was finally allowed to attend school with her sister and her cousins. Carrying her lunch in a pail, Laura happily set off for school. She was a good student from the start. Laura had been brought up in a house where books and reading were an important part of life. Ma often read aloud to the family at night from books such as *Norwood, Millbank, General Ben Butler of New Orleans,* and *The Land and the Book,* a story about Jerusalem.

The Ingallses remained in the Big Woods for three years. Pa farmed and hunted, making sure there was plenty of fresh meat to last the family through the winter. A bear could provide the family with food for a long while. The Wisconsin winters were so cold that the bear meat would hang frozen solid in a shed near the log cabin. If Ma wanted meat for dinner, Pa would chop off a chunk with his ax.

When they were not in school, Laura and Mary spent most of their time with their mother. There were always chores to be done. Ma had a special chore for each day of the week: "Wash on Monday, iron on

Tuesday, mend on Wednesday, churn on Thursday, clean on Friday, bake on Saturday, rest on Sunday."[1]

Sundays were Laura's least favorite day. There was no church for the family to attend in the Big Woods of Wisconsin. The girls were bathed in a wash-tub filled with melted clean snow in the winter or spring water in the summer. They had to put on their best dresses and hair ribbons. Then they had to sit. Ma read stories aloud from the Bible. The girls could look at pictures or sit with their rag dolls. They were not allowed to do anything else.

Sometimes Laura found it impossible to behave on Sundays. Then she would run around the cabin, shouting and playing noisily with Jack the dog. But soon her father would scold her, and Laura would have to sit quietly again.

The routine of Laura's life was occasionally broken up by large get-togethers with her relatives in the town of Pepin. It was a seven-mile trip. When Laura saw the town for the first time, she was so excited that it was difficult to breathe: "Laura had never imagined so many houses, and they were so close together. . . . She looked and looked, and could not say a word."[2]

Pepin was growing, as was the population of the entire Big Woods district. This made Pa restless. By October 1873, Pa had sold his land to Andrew Anderson for $1,000. Pa wanted to leave Wisconsin and try his luck out west again. This time, he was looking beyond the Mississippi River to Minnesota. He was eager to return to the prairie.

With the covered wagon packed once more, Laura

and her family moved in with Grandma and Grandpa Ingalls, Uncle Peter, and Aunt Eliza until they would begin their journey. Peter, Eliza, and their children would be going with them.

While the families were getting ready, Mary attended school with her cousins Alice and Peter. Laura was not allowed to go. She had to stay home to keep her cousins Ella and Edith company. Occasionally, though, she was allowed to sit in the sled while Mary pulled her through the snowy woods to the schoolhouse.

During the winter, all the children came down with scarlet fever, an illness that causes a fever and a rash. The trip was postponed until everyone had recovered. By February, Pa could wait no longer. It was essential that they travel while the ice on Lake Pepin was frozen solid.

The two families set out in their covered wagons. Saying good-bye to their grandparents, aunts, uncles, and cousins, they began the trip west.

# 4

# Walnut Grove

The wagon crawled west through Wisconsin and across Lake Pepin, which was completely frozen during the winter months. On the other side of the lake lay Minnesota. There, Pa and his brother Peter had their families camp out in an empty cabin until the weather became warmer.

Before long, the trees were sprinkled with green leaves and Pa became anxious to move on. Peter, however, decided to stay in eastern Minnesota. He had found a farm near the Zumbro River, where he would settle.

Laura and her family made their way slowly across the open prairie. Their wagon finally arrived in Walnut Grove, Minnesota, in the spring of 1874. It was a new town, composed of twenty-four blocks of wide streets.

Where the town ended, the prairie began with its tall grasses, colorful wild flowers, rich soil, and endless sky. Railroad tracks ran north of Walnut Grove, and trains often stopped there.

The Ingalls family heard of a homestead that was for sale for $430. There was even a place for them to live. It was a dugout, a home that was actually "dug out" of the bank along Plum Creek.

The dugout had one room, dirt walls, and a window opening that was covered with a small piece of greased paper. The roof was made of willow boughs with sod on top. When Laura walked up the path around the house, she was able to stand on the grassy roof. It looked just like part of the prairie.

The homestead was north of the railroad, about two miles from town. Neighboring farms were scattered about, owned by settlers from Scotland, Sweden, Norway, Ireland, England, and Canada.

Elick Nelson, who had come from Norway, was one of the first to move into the area. Like the Ingallses, his family lived along Plum Creek. When Nelson needed help with his harvest, Pa was only too glad to work for him.

Every day, Pa followed Plum Creek to Nelson's farm. He hoped to use the money he earned to buy a cow. That way, the family would always have fresh milk and butter.

Sometimes Laura walked to the Nelson's farm after she had finished her chores. She became friends with Mrs. Nelson, and with her daughter Anna.

Laura and Mary spent much of their time helping Ma with chores. They also attended school in Walnut

*Many pioneers built sod dugouts on the frontier. This family lived on the Great Plains of Nebraska.*

Grove. Only two miles away, it was close enough for Laura and Mary to walk. The sisters walked in their bare feet unless the weather was cold. Like most pioneer families, the Ingallses did not have enough money to afford shoes year-round.

The girls carried schoolbooks from home. Students at that time all brought their own books with them. Laura and Mary used the books their mother had studied from years before—one was for spelling, one for reading, and one for arithmetic.

Laura enjoyed school and was good at her lessons. At recess, she liked playing with the other children who also lived outside town on homesteads. But there was one girl Laura did not like—Nellie Owens. Nellie was the spoiled daughter of a store owner. She lived in town and made fun of Laura for wearing plain dresses and walking barefoot.

One day, Laura got her revenge.

She invited Nellie to a party and suggested they wade in Plum Creek. There, she lured Nellie into a part of the creek that was filled with mud . . . and leeches. The leeches, or "bloodsuckers," stuck to Nellie's legs and the girl screamed. Laura just laughed. She felt Nellie deserved it.

Now that the Ingalls family lived near a town, they were able to attend church on Sundays. Finding a minister was a problem—not just for the residents of Walnut Grove, but for most frontier townsfolk. They were always on the lookout for a clergyman who would be able to deliver Sunday sermons as well as officiate at baptisms, weddings, and funerals. Without a minister, settlers would often meet in one another's homes and take turns reading from the Bible.

There were ministers who traveled throughout the Midwest, rotating among several different churches each week. These part-time ministers, called circuit riders, usually traveled on horseback with saddlebags containing their necessary possessions. They lodged with families in the congregations. The ministers were supposed to be paid, but rarely did this take the form of cash. Instead, they usually wound up receiving fruits, vegetables, flour, meat, or hay.

Edwin H. Alden was the minister who traveled to Walnut Grove. Sent by the Home Missionary Society, Reverend Alden was a minister with the Congregational Church in eastern Minnesota. He traveled throughout the prairie, offering his services wherever pioneers could meet. Sometimes he held Sunday services in schoolhouses, in the homes of settlers, or even at railroad depots.

Laura first attended Reverend Alden's services at a private home. This was the beginning of the town's Union Congregational Church. Both Ma and Pa were baptized during one of these services, and Pa became a trustee of the church.

Reverend Alden—who nicknamed Laura, Mary, and Carrie his "country girls"—was not available to deliver sermons every week.[1] Still, Sunday school was held even in his absence, and Laura enjoyed it. The girls put on their best dresses and learned verses from the Bible. They also sang. Laura was especially happy that her mother was able to borrow books from the Sunday school library. Now she would have more books to read.

For most pioneer families, the church played an important role in their lives, for both religious and social reasons. Isolated as the settlers were from one another, church brought them together at least once a week. For pioneer women like Ma, the church represented civilization in what was often a very uncivilized lifestyle.

Not long after the Ingallses' arrival, the Walnut Grove residents decided to build a church. It is not known whether Pa, an excellent carpenter, helped in the construction. Most frontier churches were plain structures of logs, bricks, or sod. The benches had no backs, and the minister's pulpit was made of leftover planks of wood. The Walnut Grove church was built on the corner of Fourth and Washington Streets.

When a collection was made to buy bells for the church, Pa donated $26.15, a large sum of money for a man who had little to spare. Laura could hear the ringing of the church bells even from her homestead two miles away.

Laura later wrote of attending church a few days before Christmas. A decorated tree stood inside. Laura had never seen one before. She grabbed Mary's hand and stared.[2] Not only were there streamers on the tree, but there were gifts under it. Members of Reverend Alden's home congregation had donated presents for the pioneers. Laura received mittens, candy, a jewel box, and a fur cape and shawl. The clothing had been worn before, but Laura did not mind. Rarely had she received much more than a stick of candy at Christmas.

The Ingallses' first winter in Minnesota was a typically hard one. Blizzards seemed to blast down onto the prairie from skies that had been clear blue only minutes before. Pioneers like Laura's family were often forced to stay in their homes, bundled in coats and blankets as they gathered around the fireplace. The snow could drift up to eight feet deep in a matter of two days.

Pa needed all his strength to push open the door of their dugout each morning. As soon as there was a large enough opening, he would shove his hand through and begin clearing away the snow.

In the spring of 1875, Pa built his family a house on the opposite side of Plum Creek. It was made of wood, with real glass windows and china doorknobs. Pa did not yet have the money to pay for the supplies, but he had planted acres and acres of wheat. Once he harvested and sold the wheat, he would be able to pay for the materials. He even bought Ma an iron cookstove so she would not have to prepare meals over an open fire.

The wheat was growing well. Pa was hopeful he might even have some money left over after paying off his debts. Then, a week before Pa was going to harvest the wheat, the sky turned a strange color and a large cloud appeared overhead. It was not a usual cloud filled with rain.

Laura was staring up at the sky when suddenly something struck her head. It was a large brown locust, a kind of grasshopper. The sky was filled with them.

"They looked like a great, white glistening cloud," said one pioneer.[3]

Laura later wrote about the experience. She tried

to beat them off, but their "claws clung to her skin and her dress. . . . Grasshoppers covered the ground, there was not one bare bit to step on. Laura had to step on grasshoppers and they smashed squirming and slimy under her feet."[4]

The weight of the insects snapped tree limbs and flattened cornstalks. They piled up on the ground until they were at least four inches deep. They ate everything. Not only were the fields of wheat, corn, and vegetables destroyed, but the grasshoppers ate fences, quilts, kitchen utensils, and curtains. They even ate clothing as they landed on men, women, and children.

"I saw their bodies choke the waters of Plum Creek, I saw them destroy every green thing on the face of the earth. . . . There are unforgettable pictures of those grasshoppers in my mind," Laura wrote.[5]

The devastation continued for days. Then it was finally over. The grasshoppers had moved on, leaving the brown stains of their saliva everywhere and polluting ponds, streams, and wells with their waste. The prairie grass was gone; all the fields were stripped clean. Everything Pa had worked for was lost.

Wearing tattered boots, Pa walked two hundred miles east to find work. He could not afford to take the train. Elick Nelson helped Ma with the work that needed to be done while Pa was gone. He brought the family provisions from town and helped chop wood.

Pa returned home in the fall. The money he earned helping to harvest crops in eastern Minnesota allowed the Ingalls family to hold out for another year.

He soon found work in town, although it is not certain whether he took on jobs as a carpenter or helped out in one of the stores. He moved the family into town for the winter. Ma had given birth to another baby in November—a boy, Charles Frederick, nicknamed Freddie—and it would be easier to provide for the girls and an infant son in town during the long winter months.

The winter, however, proved to be mild. Even before the snow and ice had melted, the Ingallses moved back to Plum Creek. Pa planted more wheat that spring of 1876, hopeful that this time he would be rewarded.

Yet he did not realize that as the grasshoppers had been eating the summer before, they were also laying eggs. These eggs hatched the following summer. For the second year in a row, the Minnesota prairie was covered with hordes of grasshoppers destroying everything in sight.

Many people were leaving the area. They could not afford to stay. William Steadman and his wife decided to head to Burr Oak, Iowa, to run a hotel they had bought. Steadman asked Pa to move there with him and help manage the hotel.

Pa sold his land to Abraham and Margaret Keller and packed up the covered wagon again. Before going to Iowa, the Ingallses would stop in eastern Minnesota to visit Uncle Peter and Aunt Eliza on their farm. There, Pa could help work in the fields.

Laura and her family got into the wagon and began their journey. This time, though, they were heading east.

# Hard Times

The journey to Burr Oak, Iowa, was not a happy one. In fact, it felt like a miserable ordeal. Everything started out well enough. The family had broken up the trip from Walnut Grove by spending some time with Uncle Peter and Aunt Eliza at their home along the Zumbro River in eastern Minnesota. Their children, Peter, Alice, Ella, Edith, and baby Lansford, were good companions for the Ingalls girls.

Laura especially enjoyed going to the pasture each day and bringing the cows home to be milked. It was wonderful being outdoors amid the wildflowers, playing in the creek, and observing all the different animals that lived in the meadow.

*This is the earliest known photograph of Laura, right, and her sisters Mary, center, and Carrie.*

"Bringing home the cows is the childhood memory that oftenest recurs to me," Laura once said.[1]

Laura, Peter, and Ella were in charge of keeping the cows away from the hay that had been cut and stacked. Whenever it rained, the children found a sheltered place and built a fire. There, they roasted meat and crab apples. Mary and fourteen-year-old Alice helped their mothers prepare meals and take care of the babies.

These pleasant days soon came to an end. In late August, Laura's baby brother Freddie became ill and died at the age of nine months. He was buried near South Troy, Minnesota. The family was grief stricken. Laura did not write about this painful incident in her *Little House* books. In fact, the years from 1875 to 1879 were so filled with hardships that she completely left them out of her series.

At the close of the summer, the Ingalls family once again climbed into the wagon. They needed to reach Burr Oak by the fall.

A cold rain fell continuously. As the wagon creaked along, Ma barely spoke. The Ingallses made their way along the dirt roads. A few miles over the Iowa state line, they reached their destination.

Burr Oak was a small town. No railroad ran through it, and only about two hundred people lived there. Several years earlier, it had been the scene of a lot of activity as hundreds of pioneers passed through the area daily on their way west. But the year was now 1876—Laura was nine—and the droves of pioneers heading west had slowed since the boom of the 1840s and 1850s.

There were two hotels in Burr Oak: the American House, where the stagecoach stopped, and the Burr Oak House. The Steadmans had purchased the Burr Oak House, a two-story building with a wide front porch. It had been built twenty-five years earlier and had had numerous owners. The last person to own the hotel was William Masters, so some people referred to it as the Masters Hotel. This is where Laura and her family would live.

On the hotel's lower level were the kitchen, dining room, and a place for sleeping. The main level included a parlor with a bedroom, the hotel office, and a barroom. There were four small bedrooms upstairs.

Back in Walnut Grove, Steadman had asked Pa to help him run the hotel. In return, Pa would receive a share of the profits and rooms for his family. Pa took on another job as well, helping J. H. Porter manage a grinding mill. Ma helped Mrs. Steadman cook, clean, and do the laundry.

Laura and Mary had chores in the hotel, too. They were responsible for making the beds, washing dishes, and waiting on tables. Laura was also frequently asked to go behind the hotel to the springhouse, a small building located over a brook where dairy products and meat could be kept cool all year long. Laura would get butter and milk from the springhouse and bring it back to the hotel. The sisters also took care of little Tommy Steadman, who cried all the time. Laura did not like this job at all, although Mrs. Steadman promised to give the girls something nice at Christmas as a way of thanking them.

Neither Pa nor Ma was pleased to have a barroom

so close by. They did not like the fact that men were drinking and singing loud, raucous songs.

Laura was excited by the discovery of a bullet hole in the dining room door. She learned the story of the bullet hole from Amy, a daily worker in the hotel. The son of the hotel's former owner shot a hole in the door when he was drunk. His wife had slammed the door as she was running away from him. Although the children enjoyed the story, Pa and Ma did not.

One of the boarders in the hotel, B. L. Bisby, gave Laura singing lessons. Laura did not want these lessons. But Bisby was a regular boarder, and Laura was told she must do what he said. She had to sing scales day after day. Laura was not happy about this. She would rather have been outside playing.

Near the hotel was the Burr Oak school. It was made of brick and had two rooms. There was one teacher in each room, Sarah Donlan for the lower grades—which included Laura and Mary—and William Reed for the higher grades. Laura knew Reed because he boarded at the Burr Oak House. He was also principal of the school and an actor.

Schoolteachers at that time had a difficult job. Students were sometimes older than their teachers; they could be bigger, too. Discipline was not an easy matter. When students did not behave in class, they might be beaten with a cane or have the soles of their feet whipped. Sometimes teachers hit the students' hands with a leather strap. Occasionally, the strap was heated and then applied to the students' wet hands, making it even more painful. Students who did not answer questions correctly had to wear cone-shaped dunce caps as punishment. They had to sit on a dunce bench or stand in front of the class.

Parents believed men were better at handling the unruly students. For this reason, male teachers were preferred to female. If a teacher could not discipline his students, he was sent away.

The Burr Oak students included a handful of large, older boys who spent much of their time working on the farms in the area. They were not interested in doing schoolwork and preferred disrupting the class. They bragged that they would drive William Reed out of the school by Christmas.

The leader of the gang was a boy named Mose. When Mose came to school late one morning, Reed asked him to come to the front of the room. Mose approached Reed's desk, hoping for a fight. Reed quickly grabbed Mose's collar and tripped him. The boy landed over the teacher's knees, and Reed beat him with a ruler. The class laughed. When Mose was finally allowed to get up, he left the school—forever.

It was quieter downstairs in Sarah Donlan's room. There, Laura and Mary learned to sing the multiplication tables to the tune of "Yankee Doodle." It was common for children to learn both numbers and letters to tunes of different songs.

Christmas did not turn out to be a very happy time for Laura's family that year. Mrs. Steadman never gave the girls anything for taking care of Tommy. Also, Laura, Mary, and the Steadman boys all came down with the measles.

In January 1877, Pa moved the family out of the hotel and over to the second floor of the grocery store building, which was next door. The rooms were larger there, although the steps leading upstairs were right next to the saloon.

The following month, Laura and Mary were promoted to a higher grade, and Reed became their teacher. Laura enjoyed her reading lessons, which included the poems "The Pied Piper," "Paul Revere's Ride," and "The Village Blacksmith."

"We liked our reading lessons very much and used to practice reading them aloud at home nights," said Laura. "Pa knew, but did not tell us until later, that a crowd used to gather in the store beneath to hear us read."[2]

Laura's parents had never been comfortable having the children living so near a saloon. Also, Ma was expecting another baby. So that spring, Pa rented a house from the singing teacher, who was still boarding at the hotel. The house stood near the Congregational Church and was far more peaceful than the family's apartments.

Laura stayed home from school during May because her mother was about to have another baby. Laura was needed to help around the house. She took this opportunity to learn her multiplication tables. Even though she was an excellent student otherwise, Laura found them nearly impossible to memorize. She finally mastered them not long after her sister Grace was born on May 23.

Laura spent the summer caring for the baby and bringing in the cows. She also spent time with a friend from school, Alice Ward.

One day, one of the Ingallses' neighbors, Mrs.

Starr, approached Ma and asked if she could adopt Laura. This was not an unusual request at that time. Often, families that were short of money felt their only option was to have their children raised by someone else. Mrs. Starr was the wife of a doctor, and her daughters were grown and had moved away. She was lonely and thought Laura would make a good companion as well as help with the housework.

Laura worried that her mother would agree to this arrangement and nervously waited while Mrs. Starr described her plan.

"But Ma smiled at me and said she couldn't possibly spare me," Laura wrote. "So Mrs. Star[r] went away looking very disappointed."[3]

Business was slow at the Burr Oak House, and the Steadmans decided to sell the hotel. It was purchased by William McLaughlin, who planned to turn it into a general store.

Pa, too, was looking to move on. He had many debts. Although he had left Minnesota to find work and earn money, he decided to head back to Walnut Grove. They had been gone for a year, and they would try living there again. The songs coming from Pa's fiddle now were happy ones—"The Arkansas Traveler" and "The Star-Spangled Banner." His spirits were high, as they always were when the wagon was heading west.

The wagon was packed, and Laura took her place in the back. Like her father, she was content to be on the move again.

"Everything came at us out of the west," wrote Laura, ". . . storms, blizzards, grasshoppers, burning

*Like the pioneers in this photograph, Laura and her family were often on the move.*

hot winds and fire. . . . Yet it seemed that we wanted nothing so much as we wanted to keep on going west."[4]

It was the fall of 1877; Laura was ten. The Ingalls family felt as if they were going home.

Their welcome was a warm one when they arrived in Walnut Grove. They spent the first night with the Ensign family, their friends from the Congregational Church. One night turned into a few months, as the Ensigns suggested the Ingallses move in with them through the winter. Once warm weather returned, Pa could build a new house. In the meantime, it seemed like the ideal solution.

The Ensigns had three children—Willard, Anna, and Howard. They all went to school together, although Willard and Anna were further along in their school books than Laura or Mary.

The families got along well together. Pa contributed to the household expenses with money he earned working in a store. Ma helped with the cooking and cleaning.

Howard liked Laura and asked her if she would marry him in a few years when they were older. Laura agreed to think about it. One day, Howard began crying jealously when he saw Laura playing with the new minister's son. Laura was disgusted and told Howard she would never consider marrying him.

It was true that Laura preferred spending time with the boys at recess, rather than the girls. She enjoyed playing tag, running races, and taking part in snowball fights. She said there was only one boy in school who could throw a baseball farther than she could.

Mary did not approve of her sister's unladylike behavior. One day at recess, she grabbed Laura's hair to prevent her from running outside to join a snowball fight. Laura continued toward the schoolhouse door, pulling Mary along behind her. Both girls were pelted with snowballs. When Mary let go, Laura raced to join the others.

Laura continued to be an excellent student. On days when she was unable to attend school, she put aside time to study. Spelling was one of her best subjects, and she was often the winner in school spelling bees.

On Friday nights, the entire town became involved

in the competition to determine the best speller of the week. The Friday Night Spelling Bee was held in the schoolhouse. Parents and children walked through town, holding lanterns to light their way. The children sat at their desks while the parents found seats against the walls.

When the teacher shook the bell, the contest began. The children would line up in two rows—the two best spellers each got to choose their team. The teacher said a word out loud to each child. If the child misspelled the word, he took his seat. Eventually, only two students were left standing. The teacher continued giving them words until one of the children made a mistake. The other child was the winner.

Samuel D. Masters, William Masters's brother, became Laura's teacher during the spring term. Laura did not like him. She said he had bad teeth and bad breath, and he stood with his face only inches from hers when speaking. She especially did not like the way he held a girl's hand when he talked to her.

One day, Laura carefully held a pin between her fingers. When Mr. Masters reached for her hand, the pin pricked him. That was the last time he tried to hold Laura's hand.

Laura's independent spirit was emerging in other ways as well. Two cliques had formed among the girls at school. One was led by Nellie Owens and the other by Genevieve Masters, the teacher's daughter. Laura had disliked Nellie since the first time she lived in Walnut Grove. She quickly learned to dislike Genevieve—called Genny—who spoke with an annoying lisp and cried when she did not get her way.

Both Nellie and Genny tried to persuade Laura to join their cliques, but Laura refused. Nellie brought Laura gifts, such as hair ribbons, from her father's store. Genny invited Laura home after school and gave her cookies fresh from the oven. Laura held her ground, though. As a child, and later as an adult, Laura resisted doing what other people expected her to do—unless she also thought it was right. She played with anyone she wanted, whenever she wanted.

Gradually, Laura was surprised to find that all the girls—even Nellie and Genny—were looking at *her* as their leader. She had done nothing to seek out this honor.

By spring, Pa had earned enough money to build a house. He had worked hard through the winter as a carpenter and also helping out William Masters, who had opened a hotel in Walnut Grove. He was finally able to pay off the $2.10 in taxes that he had owed from the first time the family lived in Walnut Grove.

Pa now bought land behind the Masters hotel. In that big pasture, he built a small house. The family had gotten along well with the Ensigns, but it was very nice having their own space again.

Pa also decided to open a butcher shop in town. During the winter, the townspeople ran out of meat that they had cured and preserved, so Pa did well in his shop.

Laura took a job at the hotel that summer. She helped Emeline Masters wash dishes, sweep, dust, and make beds. She also cared for the family's young granddaughter. Laura earned fifty cents a week. Often, she had time on her hands while the baby slept. Laura found copies of the *New York Ledger* and read stories about evil villains and beautiful ladies, secret caves, and wonderful treasures.

When school started up the following winter, Laura once again had a new teacher. David M. Thorpe replaced Sam Masters. Thorpe was a lawyer. His business was slow, so he taught school. Laura preferred him to Sam Masters.

The family went to the Union Congregational Church, just as they had when they first lived in Walnut Grove. Laura attended Sunday school there in the mornings and also went to Sunday school at the Methodist Church in the afternoon. Mary was not feeling well that winter, so usually Laura went alone.

Laura enjoyed going to the Methodist Church because each week there was a contest to see which child could repeat from memory certain Bible passages. There were 104 of these verses, and they had to be recited in order and without any mistakes. Similar to a spelling bee, the contest eliminated each child who made a mistake. At the end of the year, only Laura and Howard Ensign remained in the competition. Both children recited the verses correctly and in order.

The prize was to be a reference Bible. Unfortunately, there was only one prize and two winners. The preacher's wife told Laura that she would send away for a fancier Bible with a clasp if Laura would wait for it. Laura agreed. When she finally received her Bible, she put her name in it and wrote the year: 1878. She held on to that Bible her whole life.

Laura spent some of her time babysitting that year. Many citizens of Walnut Grove had joined the Good Templar Society and needed Laura to watch their children when they attended meetings. The Good Templar Society was an organization that supported the temperance movement. Those who favored temperance wanted people to stop drinking. They wanted the sale of alcoholic beverages to be banned. During the late 1800s, the temperance movement had begun to grip the nation. Along with other Walnut Grove residents, Ma and Pa joined the fight against selling alcoholic beverages.

Laura was also hired during the winter to stay with Sadie Hurley, Mrs. Masters's daughter, who lived two miles from town. Sadie needed someone to look after her for two weeks because she was not well. Laura accepted the job, although she was horribly homesick. She brought her school books with her, so she could continue studying while she was away. She knew the money she earned would help her family, but she missed home terribly.

The winter of 1878 was a hard one in Minnesota. Blizzards repeatedly swept across the prairie. Laura, Mary, and Carrie were unable to attend school. Three children who lived on a farm outside Walnut Grove were found buried in a snowdrift, frozen to death. They had left their home during a storm and had been unable to find their way back.

In the spring, Pa began working as a store clerk. Laura, now twelve, helped care for another of Mrs. Masters's daughters. Young as she was, Laura was a mature and responsible girl, and the people of the town recognized that. They trusted her to do a variety of odd jobs, such as babysitting and running errands. Laura was proud to be able to contribute to her family's income.

In the winter of 1879, Mary became very sick. She had a pain in her head and a very high fever. The doctors called it brain fever. It was later diagnosed as a stroke, which means that a blood vessel in the brain has ruptured. Laura recalled noticing one day that one side of Mary's face seemed pulled out of shape.

Ma cut off Mary's hair to keep her cooler. For many days, the family worried that Mary would die. Eventually, the fever left and Mary began to recover. But as her body grew stronger, her eyes grew weaker. Each day, she saw less and less until she was completely blind. The last thing Mary saw was her sister Grace's blue eyes as Grace stood near a chair where Mary was sitting.

Mary accepted her blindness without complaint. Pa talked to Laura, explaining that Laura must now serve as Mary's eyes. For the rest of the years that she lived at home with her family, Laura learned to describe the sights and activities going on around them. She did this so vividly that Mary could see the images in her mind.

Pa had begun thinking about moving west again. Ma, however, did not want to move anymore. She liked being in a settled town where the girls could go to school and the family could attend church.

Yet homesteads could be had so cheaply in the West, and the open prairie was what Pa craved. He dreamed of miles of farmland with no other houses as far as the eye could see.

Still, he had no money. The little he had earned in recent years had to be used to meet the family's needs. Nothing had been saved. Pa wanted to move west, yet he could not figure out a way to do it.

The answer came soon after Mary had begun to recover from her fever. One day, Pa's sister Docia

*Both dreams and hardships drove Laura's family to crisscross the Midwest in search of a better life.*

arrived from Wisconsin in a horse and buggy. She asked her brother if he would like a job working in Dakota Territory for the railroad.

Railroads played a huge role in opening up the West to settlement. In the Dakota Territory, towns sprang up along the railroad line as it moved from Minnesota to the Missouri River. Farmers benefited from living near the railroad, because it provided a way for them to get their crops to market. Railroad companies advertised, trying to encourage people from the East to buy homesteads along these routes in the western frontier.

"Rich Farming Lands! On the Line of the Union Pacific Railroad!" read one advertisement. "Located in the Great Central Belt of Population, Commerce and Wealth, and adjoining the World's Highway from Ocean to Ocean. 12,000,000 Acres!"[5]

Docia's husband was a contractor for a railroad. In his railroad camp, there was a company store that sold a variety of goods to the workers. Would Pa be interested in managing the store?

Pa was excited by his sister's offer. Here was a chance to move west. Managing the store would allow him to earn $50 a month. He could then be a homesteader and farm the land.

Although Ma was not eager to pull up stakes again, she agreed. But she made Pa promise that this would be last time. Pa sold his house the very next day to William Masters. He would go alone first to the railroad camp. As soon as he could, he would send for the family.

Laura helped her mother get ready for the move.

*For a while, Pa would be running a store that sold food and supplies to railroad workers. The men were laying tracks to expand train service into the West.*

They received letters from Pa, containing money. After a while, he wrote to tell the family they should use the money to buy train tickets to Tracy, Minnesota. That was where the railroad line ended. Pa would meet them there.

Laura served as Mary's eyes on the train, describing what she saw inside the train as well as the scenery flashing by their windows. In Tracy, the family stayed briefly in a hotel until Pa arrived with the wagon.

They would leave Minnesota and enter Dakota Territory. There, by the Big Sioux River, they would find the railroad camp. Their new home would be on the wide, untamed prairie.

# A Prairie Winter

The part of the country where Laura's family was headed attracted thousands of pioneers in the late 1800s. It seemed as if everyone was eager to find a homestead. Advertisements claimed the land was easy to farm. More important, it was cheap.

Pa never unpacked the wagon when they pulled up to the railroad camp on the Big Sioux River. The railroad workers were ahead of schedule and had already laid track across the river. The shanties that housed the men were being taken down and the equipment dismantled. The crew was moving west.

Pa guided the wagon about forty miles west to Silver Lake. The Ingalls family soon moved into one of the railroad shanties while Pa went to work in the company store. The railroad men were basically alone on the vast prairie, far from any town or settlement. So the store offered a wide variety of goods—overalls, boots, bread, corn, nails.

Laura spent her time close to home. Ma did not want the girls to mingle with the rough men working on the railroad line. Occasionally, though, Pa took Laura with him to watch the construction crew laying the tracks. But most of her time was spent helping her mother with the chores and caring for her two younger sisters.

When she could, Laura visited with her cousin Lena. The same age as Laura, Lena was usually busy with her mother, Laura's Aunt Docia, cooking meals for the hungry railroad workers. When both girls were free, they took walks on the grassy prairie and went horseback riding.

The construction crew was able to finish the track by December. Then they began packing up and leaving the area. Lena, Aunt Docia, and Uncle Hiram also moved on. Laura's family stayed on at the deserted camp. The head surveyor of the railroad company had asked Pa if he would move into the surveyors' house for the winter and guard the property and tools that were left there. The Ingalls family would be able to live in the house for free and have access to its supply of food and coal.

During that winter, Laura helped her mother with chores, played games, and danced with her sisters while Pa played polkas and waltzes on his fiddle. The family was pleased when neighbors arrived. Robert

*At first, the only building in De Smet was the surveyors' house. The Ingalls family stayed there when they first moved to Dakota Territory. Now it is a historical site.*

and Ella Boast had filed a claim on a homestead near Silver Lake. They lived in one of the railroad shanties.

Remembering his promise to Ma that the family would not move again, Pa had also decided to settle in the area. He quickly filed a claim on a 160-acre tract near the town that would become De Smet, South Dakota. Although not many pioneers had come to the area yet, Pa was certain there would be a rush for land in the spring.

Settlers did flock to the area in the spring, attracted by all that available land. Because the house where Laura's family lived was the only building, people came to them looking for food and shelter. Ma charged twenty-five cents for a meal and another twenty-five cents to sleep on the floor near the stove.

Laura helped Ma with the meals. They baked biscuits and beans, fried potatoes and salt pork, and brewed tea. One of the visitors to stop by the Ingalls "hotel" was Reverend Alden from Walnut Grove. He was traveling west, following the railroad line and establishing Congregational churches along the way. He held the first church service in the soon-to-be-founded town of De Smet at the surveyors' house, where the Ingalls family lived. Ma recorded the date: February 29, 1880.

The town sprang up quickly. Carrie remembered looking out on where De Smet was to be situated and seeing dozens of stakes sticking out of the ground. They were marking the spots where houses, stores, a church, and a schoolhouse would be.

Pa built two stores in town. He sold one of them and kept the other, which was located across the street from Fuller's Hardware. In April, the surveyors returned, and Laura's family had to leave the large house. They moved into town and lived in Pa's new building.

Laura was eager to settle on her family's homestead. "I would rather be out on the prairie with the grass and the birds and Pa's fiddle," she wrote. "Yes, even with wolves! I would rather be anywhere than in this muddy, cluttered, noisy town crowded by strange people."[1]

De Smet continued to grow, especially when railroad tracks were laid through the town. Immigrants came by

*A family portrait: from left, Ma, Carrie, Laura, Pa, Grace, and Mary.*

the trainload, and soon there was a hotel, a saloon, a drugstore, a tailor shop, a general store, a carpentry shop, a butcher shop, a law office, a blacksmith shop, and a district court.

As soon as any threat of cold weather had passed, Pa moved the family out to the homestead that lay southeast of the town. Pa dug a well for fresh water and also planted cottonwood saplings. Some of those cottonwood trees are still standing.[2]

Laura's family stayed in a shanty that included a small cellar, with a stable nearby. The stable was dug into the side of a small hill and was made of sod, the thick mat of grass that grew on the prairie. Because timber was so scarce, sod was commonly used to build not only stables, but homes as well.

"Soddies" were well insulated—although not especially waterproof—houses. The dirt walls often turned to runny mud during rainstorms. Then the snakes that lived in the sod roof often wriggled free and dropped onto beds and tables throughout the day and night.

Money was scarce again, for Pa was spending each day working on the homestead—putting up buildings, plowing the land, and cutting the thick grass for hay. Cutting and stacking hay was a difficult task for two men, let alone one. But Pa could not afford to hire anyone to assist him.

Showing characteristic determination, Laura begged her father to let her help with the haying. She said, "I'm going on fourteen. I can help, Pa. I know I can."[3] And she did. She trampled down the loose hay until it was solid beneath her feet. She was soaked with sweat and exhausted when they finished. Together, they got the job done.

The fall of 1880 brought early blizzards to De Smet. In mid-October, the air turned bone-chillingly cold. The bitter winds were accompanied by heavy snows, drifting up to eight feet deep. One day, Pa found a neighbor's cattle with their muzzles frozen to the ground. He broke the ice off their heads to free the animals. The trains—after several days' delay because of the snow-covered tracks—continued to make it through to De Smet, bringing the townsfolk much-needed supplies.

As the winter continued and the blizzards kept up without a break, conditions became harder and more dangerous. Pa had already decided to move his family into the town until warmer weather returned. He suspected the winter would be a hard one because of the thickness of the walls of a muskrat's home. "I don't know how they know," Pa said. "But they do."[4]

Also, an elderly Indian visited the general store one day when Pa was there and warned of a particularly fierce winter.

Back in town, Laura and her sister Carrie resumed attending school. The teacher was eighteen-year-old Florence Garland, whose brother Cap (Edward) also attended classes. When Laura returned home from classes each day, she taught Mary whatever she had learned. Mary had great hopes of one day attending a college for the blind.

School was interrupted because of the continuous blizzards that winter. The storms lasted for six months, holding the prairie town in a snowy grip. By January, the trains were unable to run. The tracks were buried in snow, and no sooner did a work crew manage to dig them out than another blizzard hit. No train would be able to pass through again until May. The town was on its own—there would be no provisions brought in from the outside world.

Like most De Smet residents, Laura's family lacked food and fuel. They resorted to burning hay to keep warm. Again, Laura pleaded with her father to allow her to help twist the hay into "sticks" that they could burn.

"Laura's feet were numb from cold; they felt like wooden feet," she later wrote. "Her hands were red and when she held them in the warm air above the stove they tingled and stung and smarted where the sharp blades of grass had cut them. But she had helped Pa."[5]

These hay sticks lasted only a short time and produced very little heat. But it was all they had.

There was no oil for their lamps, and the family spent much of the time in darkness. Ma, however, was able to provide some light by crafting a lamp out of axle grease, a button, and a square of calico fabric. The flame was small, but it burned.

The only available food was wheat. Ma used an old coffee mill and took turns with her daughters grinding the wheat all day long, every day, to produce enough flour for bread.

The lines on Pa's face told how much weight he was losing. Laura felt tired and confused much of the time. The constant howling of the wind, the bitter cold, and the emptiness of her stomach made Laura feel dazed. She tried to keep up with her schoolwork while she was snowbound, but soon gave up.

"There were no more lessons. There was nothing in the world but cold and dark and work and coarse brown bread and winds blowing," she wrote. "The storm was always there, outside the walls, waiting sometimes, then pouncing, shaking the house, roaring, snarling, and screaming in rage."[6]

Sometimes the blizzards stopped for a day; sometimes for only half a day. Then, soon enough, blasts of snow and ice would beat at Laura's house again. Eventually, the town's supply of wheat ran out. Local families—including the Ingallses—were starving.

Almanzo Wilder, who had a claim on a homestead north of town, was spending the winter with his

*Almanzo Wilder proved to be a hero during the long, frozen winter.*

brother Royal in their grain and feed store not far from the Ingallses. Along with Cap Garland, Almanzo risked his life riding out into the vast, treacherously cold and snowbound prairie. There, a settler gave the men about sixty bushels of wheat, which they dragged back to town. Their brave effort allowed De Smet residents to survive the winter.

Finally, the long winter with its violent blizzards came to an end. On May 10, a train was finally able to get through. Laura later recalled receiving a barrel of Christmas gifts from Reverend Alden—it had been sitting on a snowbound train since December. Inside was a Christmas turkey, still frozen solid. Laura's parents invited Robert and Ella Boast over for Christmas dinner in May.

The Ingalls family had survived its first winter in Dakota Territory, perhaps the hardest on record. Soon, they could move back out to their homestead, back to the open prairie.

# On Her Own

Laura loved being back out on the prairie, but she also had some heavy responsibilities on her fourteen-year-old shoulders.

Ma and Pa had decided to send Mary to the Iowa College for the Blind located in the town of Vinton. Reverend Alden had told them about the school, where blind students could take courses at high school and college levels.

To help pay for Mary's tuition, Laura took a job sewing shirts at a dry goods store. She did not want to spend her time among strangers in town. Yet she was anxious to earn some money. It was hot and dusty along Main Street, but by the end of the summer, she had earned $9.

Pa and Ma took Mary to Vinton, Iowa, in the fall. At

sixteen, Mary would be studying history, chemistry, and algebra. She was also taught sewing, knitting, beadwork, and music. With her parents gone for more than a week, Laura was left to manage the homestead and take care of Carrie and Grace.

By November, the family had moved back to town for the winter, although Laura always said, "I loved the prairie and the wild things that lived upon it much better."[1]

Cap Garland's sister was no longer teaching at the school. The new teacher was Almanzo Wilder's sister, Eliza Jane. There was a new student, too. Laura was already well acquainted with her. It was Genny Masters, the girl with the lisp whom Laura had disliked in Walnut Grove. With her polite manners, Genny soon became the teacher's pet—much to Laura's dismay.

At school, Laura still joined in the boys' baseball games at recess. She also took her studies seriously and did very well, especially in history and writing. At home, when she had finished her schoolwork, she often made up poems. Sometimes they were humorous, and other times they described the beauty of the prairie in flowing verse.

Laura hoped to earn her teaching certificate when she was sixteen. Teachers were in demand on the western frontier, and Laura wanted to be able to bring in a regular salary.

De Smet was growing, and various social activities now became part of community life. There were parties called sociables, along with Friday night meetings at the schoolhouse where everyone might play charades, compete in spelling bees, or sing together.

The newly erected Congregational Church was also the scene of a lot of activity. Revival meetings were held frequently, drumming up religious excitement with songs and thunderous sermons. Although Laura attended the meetings along with many of the townsfolk, she always preferred saying her prayers in private.

Almanzo Wilder also attended these meetings. After one gathering, he asked Laura if he could walk her home. He was twenty-five and Laura was only fifteen. The walk home was a quiet one; Laura felt awkward with him and wished she could think of something to say.[2]

As the days passed, Laura and Almanzo became more comfortable with each other. Laura still admired him for the brave trip he had made with Cap Garland through the snowy prairie to bring wheat to the hungry town during the hard winter.

Laura's life changed abruptly when she was asked to teach at Brewster School, about twelve miles southwest of De Smet. Although she had not yet turned sixteen and did not have her teaching certificate, she accepted the job. She would receive $40 for teaching during the months of January and February.

The superintendent of schools tested Laura in a variety of subjects including arithmetic, geography, and English. She passed easily, and no one ever asked her age. She received her certification.

She would live with Louis Bouchie—a school

*Laura was only a teenager when she became the teacher at Brewster School. This is a replica of the original building.*

board member—and his wife, and their son. Twelve miles was too far for a daily commute.

For all her independence of spirit, Laura worried about living away from home. She also worried that she would not be successful as a schoolteacher. Her father reassured her: "You've tackled every job that ever came your way," Pa said, "You never shirked, and you always stuck to it till you did what you set out to do."[3]

In fact, Laura *was* lonely and unhappy living away from home. She found it difficult to get along with Mrs. Bouchie, who was depressed living such an isolated life. Laura did not feel welcome in their home.

She taught five students in a shanty located a half

mile away from the Bouchies' home. Teaching the small class did little to lift her spirits, but it was better than spending time in the Bouchies' house.

Laura was wretched at the thought of staying with the Bouchies for the weekend. Then, at the end of the first week, sleigh bells rang outside the schoolhouse. "It's someone for you, Teacher!" shouted one of the students.[4]

Almanzo sat in his sleigh, driving his fine pair of Morgan horses. He was waiting to take her home for the weekend. This continued throughout Laura's teaching term. Almanzo would arrive in his sleigh every Friday afternoon to pick up Laura. Then he took her back to the Bouchies' on Sundays. The frigid Dakota air made the rides uncomfortable at times, but Almanzo never failed to show up. Once, he drove her home when the temperature was forty degrees below zero. Too stiff to move, Laura had to be carried into the house, where she thawed out.

Laura had always been a straightforward girl. She wanted it understood that Almanzo was *not* her boyfriend. She pointedly told him that when she was finished teaching at the school, she would not ride with him any longer.

For once, though, Laura did not stick to her word. When she was again home living with her family, she often went riding with Almanzo in his buggy.

Laura went back to attending school herself during the week and working on Saturdays for the dressmaker in town. When she was asked to live out on a claim with the dressmaker and her daughter, Laura could not continue with her classes. The distance was too great. The law required that a claim on land be occupied a certain number of days each year. The dressmaker was afraid to be on the claim with just her daughter. Laura's presence made her feel better.

Once again, Laura had to deal with homesickness. By late spring, she returned home. Soon, Mary was back, too. She had come home for the summer from the college for the blind.

The next couple of years for Laura were filled with attending classes at school and spending time with Almanzo. His horses were well known in the area, and Laura enjoyed helping him train them, even though it was dangerous riding behind untamed animals. Together, Laura and Almanzo would ride around town at top speed behind the colts and then out onto the prairie.

Laura and Almanzo also joined a singing school. Two to three nights a week, they attended class, practicing scales and songs. Afterward, they rode in Almanzo's buggy.

Almanzo came to Laura's house on Sunday evenings, as well, where they were allowed to spend time together in the sitting room until eleven at night. Laura recalled one night when Almanzo reached up and stopped the clock just before it reached eleven. He waited until his watch told him it was midnight, and then he reset the clock to strike eleven.

That summer, Laura switched from student to teacher again. She taught at a school about four miles from De Smet.

In August, she and Almanzo decided to marry. Laura was eighteen and Almanzo was twenty-eight.

*Almanzo started courting Laura when she was fifteen years old.*
*Three years later, they were married.*

Almanzo's sister, Eliza Jane, and his mother wanted to travel to De Smet and plan a big church wedding. But neither Laura nor Almanzo liked this idea. Instead, they quickly put together a small wedding within a few days.

Laura did not even have a wedding dress. Ma helped her sew a new black dress that Laura would be able to wear again for special occasions.

They visited the town's minister on August 25, 1885. Laura asked him to omit the word *obey* from their wedding vows. "Even if I tried, I do not think I could obey anybody against my better judgment," she told Almanzo.[5]

After the ceremony, they drove to Ma and Pa's home for a dinner Ma had made. Then they headed two miles north to the homestead they would share as husband and wife.

# Moving On

Laura and Almanzo's first year of marriage began happily enough. They were living one mile outside De Smet on a homestead that was twice the size of the usual claim. Their homestead was 160 acres with an additional 160-acre tree claim about a mile away.

They intended to farm the land, and Almanzo had already planted fifty acres of wheat. Money was tight, but Laura was used to that. They had needed to buy farming equipment, purchase feed for the horses, and take out a mortgage on their gray frame house.

Laura helped Almanzo, just as she had once helped her father. She worked the farm equipment, driving a team of six horses. Their first winter together was a mild one, and the young couple had

*The parlor at Ma and Pa's home, as it looks today, with the ornate coal stove and beautiful organ.*

high hopes for the future. In December 1886, Laura gave birth to a daughter. They named her Rose, after the prairie flower.

Then the troubles came.

A hailstorm during the summer of 1887 destroyed their crops, and their debts began to mount. Then a drought made it difficult to farm the land. Before long, they had to sell half their property.

The hard times did not let up.

Next, fire destroyed the haystacks and the barn. Less than a year later, in the spring of 1888, Laura and Almanzo came down with diphtheria, a contagious disease that affects the heart and nervous system. Little

Rose was sent to stay with Ma and Pa for a few months so she would not catch her parents' illness.

Even after they recovered, Almanzo remained partially paralyzed. He had suffered a stroke during the long illness and now could not move his hands and feet without difficulty. At the age of thirty, Almanzo had to walk with a cane. Laura found herself doing a man's share of the work.

Laura had another baby in August 1889, when she was twenty-two. The infant died twenty-eight days later. Laura had not even had time to choose a name for him. Then, only two weeks after burying their son, Laura and Almanzo lost their house to a fire. A quickly made shanty became their only shelter. Drought and windstorms continued, destroying their wheat crop.

The land was parched. Laura's and Almanzo's dreams seemed to have dried up as well. They made a decision—they would travel east to Spring Valley, Minnesota, and stay with Almanzo's parents until they could get back on their feet. They would help out his parents on their farm.

In the spring of 1890, they said good-bye to Laura's family. Pa and Ma were having hard times of their own. Money was scarce, and Pa was ill much of the time. They had moved permanently to town and were living in a house Pa had built three years earlier. Finally, Ma's wish to stay in one place had become a reality. They would not move again.

Laura, Almanzo, and Rose traveled to Minnesota by covered wagon and stayed there for more than a year. Then they took a train south to Florida in the fall

*Laura and Almanzo stayed for a year at his family's home in Spring Valley, Minnesota. Almanzo is standing on the steps at the middle of the house. Laura and little Rose are seated on the porch at the right.*

of 1891. They settled in Westville, staying with Laura's cousin Peter. But Laura did not feel well in Florida. She was not used to the damp coastal climate.

Laura also felt out of place among the people of Florida. "At that time and in that place, a Yankee woman was more of a curiosity," she wrote.[1]

After a year in Florida, they returned home to De Smet, South Dakota. Initially, Laura, Almanzo, and Rose lived with Laura's family in town, but soon they moved to their own home a block away. Almanzo found work as a carpenter and a painter, while Laura went back to the dressmaker's, earning $1 a day. Ma and Mary took care of Rose while Laura worked. Rose was a bright child, and she was allowed to begin school a year early. She excelled at reading and writing. Her desire to write was so strong that she developed severe writer's cramp and had to leave school. With her parents at work, Rose spent her time with Ma and Mary.

Laura and Almanzo decided they needed to make a new life for themselves. They wanted a milder climate that would be better for Almanzo's crippled feet. They settled on the Ozark Mountains in southern Missouri, an area called the Land of the Big Red Apple. Many covered wagons were headed there. In the Ozarks, they could have an orchard and perhaps try farming on a smaller scale.

They heard that farmland was cheap in Mansfield, Missouri. Laura had saved $100 from her work at the dressmaker's. It would be enough to get them started. She took the $100 bill and hid it in a small wooden writing desk. She made Rose promise never to tell anyone about the money.

Laura kept a diary of the trip they made by covered wagon to Missouri. Her first entry is dated July 17, 1894. She was twenty-seven years old. A week and a half later, she wrote of Nebraska: "Corn is killed by the hot wind. Yesterday it was 126 degrees in the shade. . . . There was a gang of horse traders on the river and we did not want to camp near them."[2]

By early August, the Wilders' wagon was rolling through Kansas. Laura wrote, "It is *terribly* dusty. We breathe dust all day and everything is covered thick with it. . . . Dust is three to five inches deep on the road and the breeze is on our backs so all the time we are in a smother of dust."[3]

They arrived in the green hills of Missouri at the end of the month, camping in the woods while they searched for a farm to buy. Laura described it as "drowsy country that makes you feel wide awake and alive but somehow contented."[4]

One mile east of Mansfield, they found what they were looking for: a farm with a log house. Apple trees were planted on four of the forty acres.

At first, Almanzo was not very impressed with their new home. "The place looked unpromising enough when we first saw it," he said.[5]

It was not like the treeless land they had left in South Dakota. This land seemed to have rocks and brush everywhere. But they both thought that "in time it could be made very beautiful," Almanzo said.[6]

However, when Laura unlocked the writing desk to get the $100 bill, the money was missing.

"They took every sheet of writing paper out of the desk and shook it," Rose said later. "They took each letter out of its envelope, unfolded it, looked into the empty envelope. They turned the desk upside down and shook it, the felt-covered inside lids flapping."[7]

For days, the money could not be found. The Wilders resigned themselves to not being able to buy the farm. Then one day, the bill turned up. It had fallen into a crack in the desk during the bouncy wagon ride.

Laura and Almanzo signed the papers to purchase

the property on September 24, 1894. They named it Rocky Ridge Farm.

The couple got busy right away. They were used to hard work. They planted a cornfield and garden, increased the size of the apple orchard, and began clearing away the rocks, brush, and timber. They built a barn and a hen house. During the first two years, they survived by selling produce from Laura's garden, eggs from the hens, and timber that Laura had helped saw.

"It was hard work and sometimes short rations at the first, but gradually the difficulties were overcome," recalled Laura.[8]

Almanzo was still unable to put in a full day's work, but Laura did far more than her share. She became an expert at sawing down trees, as well as getting her hens to lay many eggs.

Laura and Almanzo thought it might make their lives easier if they moved into town. So, still holding on to Rocky Ridge, they rented a small house in Mansfield only a mile from their farm. Here, Almanzo became a deliveryman, hauling loads in and around the town with a wagon and horses. Laura served meals from their home to travelers passing through town.

Living in Mansfield also made it easier for Rose to attend school. An outstanding student, Rose had often ridden her donkey, Spookendyke, to school from her family's farm. Rose hated the donkey, which continually bucked her off. From her house in town, Rose needed to walk only a few blocks to school. The school offered classes through eighth grade, but the Wilders did not have the money to send Rose on to high school.

As the years passed, the Wilders continued working on the farm, hoping it would one day be self-sufficient. They eventually increased its size to two hundred acres. They raised hogs, sheep, cows, and goats. Almanzo bought a Morgan horse and began breeding horses. He also built a frame house near the log cabin.

In May 1902, Laura received word that her father was dying. Pa had been suffering from heart failure for many years. She quickly left Rocky Ridge and took the train to South Dakota. Laura was at Pa's side when he died on June 8. He was buried on the prairie next to Laura's infant son.

The obituary that appeared June 12, 1902, in the *De Smet News* stated: "As a citizen he held high esteem, being honest and upright in his dealings and associations with his fellows. As a friend and neighbor he was always kind and courteous, and a faithful and loving husband and father."[9]

Laura remained in De Smet for a while to visit with her family before heading back to Missouri. It was the last time she would ever see Ma or Mary. Ma died in 1924. Mary died in 1928.

Shortly after Laura returned home, Almanzo's sister Eliza Jane came for a visit. She was now a widow living in Louisiana with a son of her own. She invited Rose to come back with her to Louisiana. There, Rose could continue her education. Rose was more than happy to leave Rocky Ridge—she had never enjoyed farm life.

*Here, in her house on Rocky Ridge Farm, Laura later wrote the* Little House *books.*

There were seven students enrolled at the high school in Crowley, Louisiana, and they were often allowed to study and recite their lessons in the principal's office. Rose did extremely well in her school work. One of the subjects she studied was Latin, and she wrote a poem in Latin for the graduation ceremony.

Rose was an independent young woman. When her schooling was finished, she learned how to operate a telegraph from an agent at a local depot. She then boarded a train for Kansas City, Missouri, and worked as a telegraph operator there. Rose was seventeen at the time, living alone, and earning $2.50 a week.

Rose remained at her job in Kansas City until 1907. She then became a manager for a Western Union telegraph office in Indiana. In the spring of 1908, she traveled to San Francisco, California, and tried her hand at journalism, becoming a feature writer for the San Francisco *Bulletin*. During this time, Rose met Gillette Lane. The two were married on March 24, 1909.

Their baby boy was born the next year, but he did not live long. Over the next few years, the Lanes moved a few times, returning finally to San Francisco, where they worked selling real estate. But they were growing apart, their marriage faltering. Rose took up writing once again.

Meanwhile, Laura was beginning to do some writing of her own. When she was in her forties, Laura was asked to speak at various agricultural meetings. She was considered an expert on raising chickens. On one occasion, Laura could not attend a meeting. She wrote down her speech for someone else to read. The editor of the farm paper *Missouri Ruralist* was there and found the speech both informative and interesting. He contacted Laura and asked her if she would send him other articles. He wanted to publish them.

In her first article, Laura talked about the rewards of living on a farm and the importance of husbands and wives working together to make their farms a success. She signed her name "Mrs. A. J. Wilder."

Laura went on to write other articles. It is unclear why, but she listed Almanzo as the author of some

*Laura's daughter, Rose, above, was becoming a well-known journalist.*

stories, such as "The Story of Rocky Ridge Farm," and "My Apple Orchard." Between 1912 and 1915, seven of her articles appeared in the *Missouri Ruralist.*

Laura became editor of the paper's "Home" column. She also began writing for other publications, such as the *Missouri State Farmer* and the *St. Louis Star.*

In 1915, Laura took a train to California to visit Rose. San Francisco was hosting a world's fair, the San Francisco International Exposition, to celebrate the opening of the Panama Canal. Laura was forty-eight, and made the journey alone. Although she was not comfortable at first with the thought of Almanzo doing the chores and looking after himself, Rose talked her into making the trip by herself.

Rose had been trying for some time to persuade her parents to move to California, where the weather was milder. During Laura's stay, Rose showed her mother possible places where she could live, such as the Santa Clara Valley. Acreage, however, was expensive, and Laura did not care for the heat, the dust, or the flat landscape.

Another purpose of the visit was for Rose to help her mother with her writing career. Rose firmly believed that Laura had the ability to be a successful writer. Laura had a talent for describing scenes, people, and events. She also had a very clear and direct style of writing.

In a September 21, 1915, letter to Almanzo, Laura wrote, "Rose and I are blocking out a story of the Ozarks for me to finish when I get home. If I can only make it sell, it ought to help a lot and besides, I am learning so that I can write others for the magazines.

If I can only get started at that, it will sell for a good deal more than farm stuff."[10]

After Laura had been in San Francisco for two months, the *Missouri Ruralist* asked her to write several articles about the exposition. Laura's feature story on Missouri's exhibits at the exposition ran on the newspaper's front page.

Laura and Rose spent much of their time in San Francisco sightseeing. They walked all over the city, visiting such places as Telegraph Hill and Fisherman's Wharf. They went to concerts and toured college campuses. Although Laura found San Francisco beautiful, she said she "would not give one Ozark hill for all the rest of the state that I have seen."[11] She had no interest in staying there permanently.

When she returned home to Rocky Ridge, Laura spent her time tending her chickens, caring for her garden, and helping Almanzo. She also began writing regularly for the *Missouri Ruralist*, and her reputation grew as a farm-paper writer.

*When she was in her forties, Laura began to try her hand at writing.*

# The *Little* *House* Books

In addition to writing, Laura became increasingly involved in clubs and local organizations. She helped set up two study groups, the Athenians and the Justamere Club. She remained active in her church and worked with an association that offered loans to farmers.

In 1917, Laura helped organize the National Farm Loan Association in Mansfield and became the secretary-treasurer. Laura was in charge of the book-keeping for the association as well as giving out loans.

Her daughter's writing career was taking off. In addition to newspaper writing, Rose also wrote stories and articles for such magazines as *The Ladies' Home Journal*, *Harper's Monthly*, *Country Gentleman*, and

*The Saturday Evening Post*. She published a book, *Henry Ford's Own Story*, in 1917.

Unfortunately, Rose's marriage was not flourishing as well as her career, and in 1918 she and her husband divorced. She wrote a novel, *Diverging Roads*, which was based on her separation and divorce.

Rose's fame as a writer would grow through the years as she traveled to New York, Paris, Vienna, Rome, and Baghdad. For a time, she served as a reporter for the American Red Cross, writing about the conditions in war-torn countries.

With Rose's encouragement, Laura, too, continued to write. She had an article published in *McCall's* in 1919, entitled "Whom Will You Marry?" For the first time, she signed her name "Laura Ingalls Wilder."

In 1924, Rose came back to Rocky Ridge Farm to live with her parents. She helped Laura turn out two articles for *The Country Gentleman*: "My Ozark Kitchen" and "The Farm Dining Room." Laura received $150 apiece for the articles.

When Rose herself sold a series of articles a few years later to the same magazine for $10,000, she used the money to build a new house for her parents. It was a five-room cottage built in the English style. Rose also had electricity put in the old farmhouse.

Laura and Almanzo were always considering additional ways to earn money. Aside from what they produced on the farm, Laura's writing helped their income. In 1925, she decided to run for political office. If elected to the position of collector for Pleasant Valley Township, she would receive a salary of $300 a year.

*Soon Laura was selling articles to popular magazines of the day.*

Running on the independent farmers' ticket, Laura put an advertisement in the *Mansfield Mirror* for several weeks announcing her candidacy. She described the kind of person she was and promised to be fair. She also mentioned her experience with the National Farm Loan Association. "I have been a busy farm woman and have not had time to do as much for the community as I would have liked to do," she stated, "but whenever possible I have done my best."[1]

In the election held on March 31, Laura finished in third place, with only sixty votes. Then, with the election behind her, Laura refocused her energies on her writing. Now in her sixties, Laura decided to write her autobiography. One day in 1930, she took a blue-lined tablet of paper and began to write down her memories of life as a pioneer girl.

"I wrote between washing dishes and getting dinner, or just any time I could. But sometimes I got stumped on a phrase or a chapter. Maybe the way to do it would not come to me until after I had gone to bed and then I would think of something in the middle of the night," she recalled.[2] Rose helped edit the manuscript, and "Pioneer Girl" was sent to Rose's agent in New York.

Laura said that the autobiography was a way of passing on her memories. "I began to think what a wonderful childhood I had had," she explained. "How I had seen the whole frontier, the woods, the Indian country of the great plains, the frontier towns, the building of railroads in wild, unsettled country, homesteading and farmers coming in to take possession. I realized I had seen and lived it all."[3]

Although publishers thought Laura's story was

interesting, no one wanted to buy it. Rose even tried to sell "Pioneer Girl" to various magazines, but she was unsuccessful. A friend of Rose's from San Francisco heard of Laura's manuscript and suggested that it might work best as a children's picture book. Several more editors took a look at "Pioneer Girl." It fell into the hands of editor Marion Fiery at Knopf Books, who found the story "delightful."[4] But she wanted to change the title to *Little House in the Woods*. Other titles that had been considered were *Trundle-Bed Tales, Little Pioneer Girl, Long Ago Yesterday,* and *Little Girl in the Big Woods.*[5]

In the middle of her excitement over the story being published, Laura was suddenly told that Knopf was closing its children's department. It was the early 1930s, and the country was mired in the Great Depression, a severe economic slump. Many businesses were closing down. Money was tight everywhere. Knopf needed to cut costs. Fiery suggested that the editors at Harper Publishers might be interested in the manuscript. And they were.

Laura's first book was published in 1932, when she was sixty-five years old. It is called *Little House in the Big Woods*. "That book was a labor of love and is really a memorial to my father," she said.[6]

Harper Publishers believed even the Great Depression would not be able to stop sales of Laura's book. And the company was right. It seemed as if instantly book reviewers were praising the story. Equally fast, her readers wanted more. So did Harper Publishers.

Throughout what came to be known as the *Little*

*House* series, Rose served as her mother's editor. "Without your fine touch, it would be a flop," Laura told Rose. "You see I know the music but I can't think of the words."[7]

The books chronicle Laura's life from the time she was a little girl in the Big Woods of Wisconsin to her married life with Almanzo. Although she occasionally changed some names and dates, the *Little House* books—for the most part—give an accurate account of Laura's life as she traveled through the unsettled West in a covered wagon.

*Little House in the Big Woods* tells the story of Laura, Mary, and Carrie living with Ma and Pa in the woods of Wisconsin. The stories in it are a combination of Laura's two stays in Wisconsin. There are tales of curing bear meat, boiling sap to make maple syrup, Pa's being chased by a panther, and young Laura's seeing a town for the first time in her life.

Laura had never expected to write more than one book. Yet there was such a great demand that she turned out seven more. In 1933, she wrote *Farmer Boy*. This book focuses on Almanzo's life growing up on a farm near Malone, in New York State. There are descriptions of Almanzo's chores, the enormous meals his family ate, his days in school, and how he trained young calves and longed to one day train horses.

Two years later, *Little House on the Prairie* was published. Returning to Laura and the Ingalls family, the book tells of their time in Kansas. Laura explained how Pa built a home for his family. She wrote of the times Indians came to visit the cabin, looking for food. She described the day the Indians left the region, and how she watched them ride away from the prairie forever.

In *On the Banks of Plum Creek*, published in 1937, the family had moved to Minnesota. Hoping to have a successful wheat harvest, the Ingallses were not prepared for the millions of grasshoppers that devastated the crops. The family eventually had to leave, but not before Laura attended school for the first time.

The character of Nellie Oleson first appeared in this book. Nellie was, in fact, based on three of Laura's acquaintances: Nellie Owens, Genevieve Masters, and Stella Gilbert. Stella lived on a farm near De Smet and was in competition with Laura for Almanzo's

*Laura's books are set in the many places she lived throughout her life.*

affections. Nellie Oleson's character would return in *Little Town on the Prairie* and *These Happy Golden Years*.

Laura chose not to include the years that were especially hard for her family in the *Little House* series, skipping tragic events such as Mary's illness and eventual blindness, and the death of baby Freddie. The Ingalls family had left Minnesota after the second summer of grasshopper invasion. They traveled to Burr Oak, Iowa, before returning to Minnesota. In *By the Shores of Silver Lake*, Laura jumped ahead to her family's move to the railroad camp in Dakota Territory. The book was published in 1939. It tells of how the Ingallses became the first settlers in the new town of De Smet.

*The Long Winter*, published in 1940, continues the story of the family's years in South Dakota. Laura described the hard winter of 1880–1881, when the town was covered in snow and had no access to the trains or any supplies from the outside world. With little food or fuel, the townsfolk of De Smet might not have survived that winter if Almanzo Wilder and Cap Garland had not made the dangerous journey across the prairie to find wheat.

Laura is a teenager in *Little Town on the Prairie*, which was published in 1941. In De Smet, she attended church socials and dances and began spending time with Almanzo. Laura also used the summer months to sew shirts to help earn money so Mary could attend a college for the blind.

The next book picks up at age fifteen, when Laura received her teaching certificate and traveled twelve miles from home to teach at a claim shanty. *These Happy Golden Years*, published in 1943, tells of Laura's homesickness as well as her determination to earn money for Mary's college education. Laura and Almanzo became even closer when he appeared in a sleigh every weekend to take her home to her family. Laura ended the *Little House* series with her marriage to Almanzo and her move away from Ma and Pa.

Laura was seventy-six when she stopped writing the series. She had never planned to write about her life after marrying Almanzo, and there did not seem to be any reason to do so. Her first seven books continued to bring in money, and after writing for more than a decade, she was ready to stop. She also did not want to write about the early years of her marriage because they were difficult and, occasionally, sad years.

In response to her books, Laura received letters from children all over the country. They made her birthday cards and Valentine's Day cards. They sent her pictures of themselves and pictures they had drawn based on the *Little House* stories. One child wrote:

"Dear Laura, Thank you. Good Books. I like them. I am seven years old. Merrill."[8]

Even though Laura was famous, she still cooked Almanzo his breakfast at seven each morning while he tended the goats and cows. "I always have been a busy person . . . but I love to work," she stated. "And it is a pleasure to write. And, oh, I do just love to play! The days never have been long enough to do the things I would like to do. Every year has held more interest than the year before."[9]

# 10

# Leaving a Mark

Laura continued to be overwhelmed with fan letters. She was not able to write many personal replies in her later years. Rheumatism, which can cause pain in the muscles and joints, had developed in her hands. Harper Publishers drew up a form letter for her to send out in addition to the personal responses she still managed to write.

Laura and Almanzo were living a quiet life now. Laura had no plans to continue her writing career, and for the most part, she and Almanzo stayed on the farm. When they went into town, they would attend church, go shopping, or visit with friends. Laura went to occasional meetings of the Women's Society of Christian Service of the Methodist Church.

Almanzo preferred spending his time at Rocky

Ridge, making furniture and carving canes out of different types of wood that he found on the farm. He also raised goats and had trained them to lift their front legs onto a stool. Because of Almanzo's bad leg, he could milk them more easily in this position. Laura, however, did not like Almanzo's use of white handkerchiefs to clean the goats' udders. She refused to wash the handkerchiefs, and Almanzo had to take them into town for laundering.

In 1939, Laura and Almanzo traveled back to De Smet for Old Settler's Day. Laura was seventy-two; Almanzo was eighty-two. She later said they recognized many faces, but she was surprised that everyone had turned "old and gray like ourselves."[1] In Laura's memory, everyone was young.

Grace died shortly after Laura's trip to De Smet, and Carrie died in 1946. Laura was the last survivor of her immediate family.

Almanzo and Laura had sold part of their farm to H. L. Shorter and his wife, Gireda, in 1943. By 1948, they made the decision to sell the rest of it because they were not able to take care of it themselves. They sold it on an installment plan for $8,000, with an agreement that they could continue living in their home at Rocky Ridge.

Almanzo's health was failing, so when the Detroit Public Library invited Laura to attend a ceremony for the opening of a new branch named in her honor, Laura did not go. She wrote a letter instead and presented the library with the original manuscripts of *The Long Winter* and *These Happy Golden Years*.

About this time, an article about Laura appeared

in the *Kansas City Star* and was reprinted in the *Mansfield Mirror*. It stated that not only had millions of Americans read her *Little House* books but that the books were being read throughout the world. It referred to Laura as a "famous author," adding that she was "unaffected and as unassuming as in her earlier days here when she helped 'pull a crosscut saw' on Ozark timber."[2]

When Almanzo was ninety-two, he suffered a heart attack. After several months of illness, he died on October 23, 1949.

Laura remained on the farm, answering children's letters and giving occasional speeches. She was also being recognized for her books. The Athenians, which Laura had helped organize many years earlier, declared a Laura Ingalls Wilder Day in August 1950 and held a tea in her honor. Some 135 people attended the festivities, which were at the Wright County Library in Hartville. Also that year, the official manual of Missouri included Laura in a section on famous people from the state.

In the spring of 1950, the public library in Pomona, California, opened its Laura Ingalls Wilder Room in the children's section. Laura donated the original manuscript of *Little Town on the Prairie*. The following year, the Mansfield branch library moved into a new building and named it the Laura Ingalls Wilder Library.

As time moved on, Laura's pace slowed. She enjoyed playing solitaire and reading. Her favorite books were detective stories and westerns, especially those by Luke Short and Zane Grey. Although she

*"I had no idea I was writing history," said Laura Ingalls Wilder. This picture shows her autograph, too.*

could still sew, embroider, and crochet, she eventually became too feeble to do any needlework.

The *Little House* series and its author continued to be honored. Five of her books won Newbery Honors. In 1954, the American Library Association created the Laura Ingalls Wilder Award to be given to special authors who had made a lasting contribution to children's literature. Laura was the first to receive the award, although she was too weak to attend the ceremony. Between 1954 and 1980, the Laura Ingalls Wilder Award was given out every five years; it is now given every three years. Past winners have included E. B. White in 1970, Theodor Geisel ("Dr. Seuss") in 1980, Maurice Sendak in 1983, and Elizabeth George Speare in 1989.

On February 10, 1957, Laura Ingalls Wilder died. She had just turned ninety. Like her husband, she was buried in Mansfield, Missouri.

Stories about Laura's experiences as a pioneer girl continued to be published even after her death. In 1962, *On the Way Home*, a diary of her trip from De Smet to Mansfield, appeared in stores.

Rose died in 1968, and *The First Four Years* was published in 1971. The manuscript for the book had been found among Laura's papers soon after her death. The shortest of the *Little House* books, *The First Four Years* was divided into four parts—one for each year of Laura's early married life. Laura told of how she and Almanzo began their marriage on the prairie and faced numerous hardships, including illness, the loss of a child, their house and crops being destroyed, and shortage of money.

In 1974, the television show *Little House on the Prairie* began a run that would last nine years. It starred Michael Landon as Pa, Karen Grassle as Ma, and Melissa Gilbert as Laura. Although the show only loosely followed the *Little House* books, it was tremendously popular.

A television movie based on Laura's years in Dakota Territory aired in January 2000. *Beyond the Prairie: The True Story of Laura Ingalls Wilder* featured Richard Thomas and Lindsay Crouse.

The stories of Laura's life began with her memories of traveling west in a covered wagon. Her lifetime spanned the development of railroads, the coming of automobiles, airplanes, movies, radio, television, and X rays, and the launching of satellites.

Laura did not want the memories of her youth to be lost. Her books have been praised throughout the years for giving readers a sense of what the pioneer days were like.

"I wanted children now to understand what is behind the things they see," she once said, "what it is that made America the way they know it."[3]

# Chronology

1867—Born in Pepin County, Wisconsin.

1868—Ingalls family moves to Missouri.

1869—Moves to Kansas.

1871—Returns to Big Woods of Wisconsin.

1874—Moves to Walnut Grove, Minnesota.

1876—Moves to Burr Oak, Iowa.

1877—Returns to Walnut Grove, Minnesota.

1879—Mary loses her eyesight; Ingalls family moves to Dakota Territory.

1885—Laura marries Almanzo Wilder on August 25.

1886—Daughter Rose is born on December 5.

1890—Wilders move to Minnesota.

1891—Move to Florida.

1892—Return to De Smet, South Dakota.

1894—Move to Mansfield, Missouri.

1912—Laura begins writing articles.

1932—First *Little House* book is published, *Little House in the Big Woods*.

1949—Almanzo dies of heart failure at home at Rocky Ridge Farm on October 23.

1957—Laura dies of heart failure at home on February 10.

1968—Rose Wilder Lane dies on October 30.

# Books by
# Laura Ingalls Wilder

*Little House in the Big Woods,* 1932

*Farmer Boy,* 1933

*Little House on the Prairie,* 1935

*On the Banks of Plum Creek,* 1937

*By the Shores of Silver Lake,* 1939

*The Long Winter,* 1940

*Little Town on the Prairie,* 1941

*These Happy Golden Years,* 1943

*On the Way Home,* 1962

*The First Four Years,* 1971

*West from Home,* 1974

# Chapter Notes

## Chapter 1. On the Move

1. Joanna L. Stratton, *Pioneer Women: Voices from the Kansas Frontier* (New York: Simon & Schuster, 1981), p. 46.

2. Andrea Warren, *Pioneer Girl: Growing Up on the Prairie* (New York: Morrow Junior Books, 1998), p. 14.

3. William Anderson, *Laura Ingalls Wilder: A Biography* (New York: HarperCollins Publishers, 1992), p. 33.

4. Laura Ingalls Wilder and Rose Wilder Lane, *A Little House Sampler* (New York: HarperCollins Publishers, 1988), p. 68.

## Chapter 2. Growing Up

1. Stephen W. Hines, *I Remember Laura: Laura Ingalls Wilder* (Nashville, Tenn.: T. Nelson Publishers, 1994), p. 68.

2. John E. Miller, *Becoming Laura Ingalls Wilder: The Woman Behind the Legend* (Columbia, Mo.: University of Missouri Press, 1998), p. 3.

3. William Anderson, *Laura Ingalls Wilder: A Biography* (New York: HarperCollins Publishers, 1992), p. 31.

4. Michael Trinklein, *The Oregon Trail*, <http://www.isu.edu/~trinmich/Hardships.html>, (October 2, 2002).

5. Laura Ingalls Wilder, *Little House on the Prairie* (New York: HarperCollins Publishers, 1935), p. 327.

6. Donald Zochert, *The Life of Laura Ingalls Wilder* (Chicago: Henry Regnery Company, 1976), p. 40.

7. Wilder, *Little House on the Prairie*, p. 290.

## Chapter 3.  Back to the Big Woods

1. Laura Ingalls Wilder, *Little House in the Big Woods* (New York: HarperCollins Publishers, 1932), p. 29.

2. Ibid., pp. 165–166.

## Chapter 4.  Walnut Grove

1. Donald Zochert, *The Life of Laura Ingalls Wilder* (Chicago: Henry Regnery Company, 1976), p. 88.

2. Laura Ingalls Wilder, *On the Banks of Plum Creek* (New York: HarperCollins Publishers, 1937), p. 251.

3. Joanna L. Stratton, *Pioneer Women: Voices from the Kansas Frontier* (New York: Simon & Schuster, 1981), p. 102.

4. Wilder, *On the Banks of Plum Creek*, p. 195.

5. Laura Ingalls Wilder and Rose Wilder Lane, *A Little House Sampler* (New York: HarperCollins Publishers, 1988), p. 220.

## Chapter 5.  Hard Times

1. Donald Zochert, *The Life of Laura Ingalls Wilder* (Chicago: Henry Regnery Company, 1976), p. 106.

2. Ibid., p. 118.

3. John E. Miller, *Becoming Laura Ingalls Wilder: The Woman Behind the Legend* (Columbia, Mo.: University of Missouri Press, 1998), p. 39.

4. Laura Ingalls Wilder and Rose Wilder Lane, *A Little House Sampler* (New York: HarperCollins Publishers, 1988), p. 29.

5. Andrea Warren, *Pioneer Girl: Growing Up on the Prairie* (New York: Morrow Junior Books, 1998), p. 10.

## Chapter 6.  A Prairie Winter

1. Laura Ingalls Wilder, *By the Shores of Silver Lake* (New York: HarperCollins Publishers, 1939), p. 254.

2. Donald Zochert, *The Life of Laura Ingalls Wilder* (Chicago: Henry Regnery Company, 1976), p. 166.

3. Laura Ingalls Wilder, *The Long Winter* (New York: HarperCollins Publishers, 1940), p. 4.

4. Wilder, *The Long Winter*, p. 12.

5. Ibid., p. 191.

6. Ibid., p. 310.

### Chapter 7. On Her Own

1. Donald Zochert, *The Life of Laura Ingalls Wilder* (Chicago: Henry Regnery Company, 1976), p. 178.

2. Ibid., p. 188.

3. Laura Ingalls Wilder, *These Happy Golden Years* (New York: HarperCollins Publishers, 1943), p. 3.

4. Ibid., p. 30.

5. Ibid., p. 270.

### Chapter 8. Moving On

1. John E. Miller, *Becoming Laura Ingalls Wilder: The Woman Behind the Legend* (Columbia, Mo.: University of Missouri Press, 1998), p. 68.

2. Laura Ingalls Wilder, *On the Way Home* (New York: HarperCollins Publishers, 1962), p. 34.

3. Ibid., pp. 50–51.

4. Ibid., p. 69.

5. Donald Zochert, *The Life of Laura Ingalls Wilder* (Chicago: Henry Regnery Company, 1976), p. 218.

6. Ibid.

7. Wilder, *On the Way Home*, p. 81.

8. Miller, p. 97.

9. Obituary for Charles Philip Ingalls: A Pioneer Gone. <http://www.vvv.com/~jenslegg/obitchar.htm> (October 2, 2002).

10. Roger Lea MacBride, ed., *West from Home* (New York: Harper & Row Publishers, 1974), p. 67.

11. Ibid., p. 117.

## Chapter 9. The *Little House* Books

1. John E. Miller, *Becoming Laura Ingalls Wilder: The Woman Behind the Legend* (Columbia, Mo.: University of Missouri Press, 1998), pp. 163–163.

2. Stephen W. Hines, *I Remember Laura: Laura Ingalls Wilder* (Nashville, Tenn.: T. Nelson Publishers, 1994), p. 101.

3. Anne Commire, ed., *Something About the Author: Facts and Pictures about Authors and Illustrators of Books for Young People* (Detroit, Mich.: Gale Research Company, 1982), vol. 29, p. 245.

4. Miller, *Becoming Laura Ingalls Wilder*, p. 185.

5. Ibid.

6. Donald Zochert, *The Life of Laura Ingalls Wilder* (Chicago: Henry Regnery Company, 1976), p. 233.

7. William Holtz, *The Ghost in the Little House: A Life of Rose Wilder Lane* (Columbia, Mo.: University of Missouri Press, 1993), p. 279.

8. *Dear Laura: Letters from Children to Laura Ingalls Wilder* (New York: HarperCollins Publishers, 1996), p. 78.

9. Stephen W. Hines, *I Remember Laura: Laura Ingalls Wilder* (Nashville, Tenn.: T. Nelson Publishers, 1994), p. 69.

## Chapter 10. Leaving a Mark

1. Donald Zochert, *The Life of Laura Ingalls Wilder* (Chicago: Henry Regnery Company, 1976), p. 238.

2. John E. Miller, *Becoming Laura Ingalls Wilder: The Woman Behind the Legend* (Columbia: University of Missouri Press, 1998), p. 256.

3. *Dear Laura: Letters from Children to Laura Ingalls Wilder* (New York: HarperCollins Publishers, 1996), p. v.

# Further Reading

## Books

Anderson, William. *Laura Ingalls Wilder Country*. New York: HarperPerennial, 1990.

———. *Laura's Album: A Remembrance Scrapbook of Laura Ingalls Wilder*. New York: HarperCollins, 1998.

Josephson, Judith Pinkerton. *Growing Up in Pioneer America: 1800 to 1890*. Minneapolis, Minn.: Lerner Publishing Group, 2002.

Wade, Mary Dodson. *Homesteading on the Plains: Daily Life in the Land of Laura Ingalls Wilder*. Brookfield, Conn.: Millbrook Press, 1997.

## Internet Addresses

**The Definitive Laura Ingalls Wilder Pages**
<http://carver.pinc.com/~jenslegg/>

**Laura Ingalls Wilder: Author of the Little House Books**
<http://www.lauraingallswilder.com>

**Laura Ingalls Wilder Historic Home and Museum**
<http://www.lauraingallswilderhome.com>

# Index

Page numbers for photographs are in **boldface** type.